Applications of Point Cloud Technology

Edited by Cumhur Şahin

Published in London, United Kingdom

Applications of Point Cloud Technology
http://dx.doi.org/10.5772/intechopen.1001660
Edited by Cumhur Şahin

Contributors
Bahadır Ergun, Cumhur Sahin, Furkan Bilucan, Hatice Cigdem Zagra Oz, Jhonattan G. Martinez, Luis A. Alarcon, Nese Atik, Ross McAree, Søren Wandahl, Tyson Phillips, Vedant Bhandari

First published in London, United Kingdom, 2024 by IntechOpen
IntechOpen is the global imprint of INTECHOPEN LIMITED, registered in England and Wales, registration number: 11086078, 167-169 Great Portland Street, London, W1W 5PF, United Kingdom

British Library Cataloguing-in-Publication Data
A catalogue record for this book is available from the British Library

Additional hard and PDF copies can be obtained from orders@intechopen.com

Applications of Point Cloud Technology
Edited by Cumhur Şahin
p. cm.
Print ISBN 978-0-85466-791-8
Online ISBN 978-0-85466-790-1
eBook (PDF) ISBN 978-0-85466-792-5

Meet the editor

Cumhur Şahin graduated as a geomatics engineer from Istanbul Technical University, Türkiye, in 2001. He received his Ph.D. from Yıldız Technical University, Geodesy and Photogrammetry Department, Türkiye, in 2011. He has been continuing his academic studies at Gebze Technical University Geomatics Engineering Department since 2001. Cumhur Şahin is currently working as an associate professor at the same university. His research interests include photogrammetry, panoramic imaging systems, optical and laser unmanned aerial vehicle studies, terrestrial laser scanning systems, 3D modeling, and documentation of cultural heritage. He has published his academic work as research articles, book chapters, and conference proceedings.

Contents

Preface

A point cloud is a collection of data points defined by a given coordinate system, typically used to represent the external surface of objects. These points, produced by various methods such as LiDAR or photogrammetric systems, provide a highly detailed and accurate three-dimensional model of physical environments. The significance of point cloud technology lies in its ability to support a wide range of applications across industries, from architecture and construction to cultural heritage preservation, autonomous systems, and beyond. By facilitating the creation of precise digital twins of real-world objects and environments, point cloud technology enables improved decision-making, enhanced project efficiency, and a deeper understanding of complex structures.

This book brings together knowledge from different disciplines, focusing on the practical applications of point cloud technology. Each chapter includes research findings and case studies performed by experts. Thus, the book serves as a valuable resource for a broad audience, including researchers, students, and professionals across various fields. It provides both theoretical knowledge and practical guidance, making it useful for anyone interested in learning about or applying this technology.

Cumhur Şahin
Geomatics Engineering,
Gebze Technical University,
Kocaeli, Türkiye

Chapter 1

Terrestrial Backpack Laser Scanner Usage in Mobile Surveying: A Case Study for Cadastral Surveying

Cumhur Sahin, Bahadır Ergun and Furkan Bilucan

Abstract

There are several different methods in laser scanning technology including terrestrial laser scanner (TLS), airborne laser scanner (ALS), and mobile laser scanner (MLS). In addition to these scanners, there are personal laser scanners (PLS). PLS are examined under two main categories as handheld personal laser scanner (HPLS) and backpack personal laser scanner (BPLS) which are the latest additions to these laser scanning technologies. Today, the use of personal laser scanner technology is a popular research and application topics. The primary advantage of PLS lies in its high mobility in different topography conditions and rapid data acquisition. Unlike TLS and MLS, the operator carries the PLS device in the work area at standard walking speed, which is sufficient to collect data. Also, PLS technology eliminates the limitations of moving TLS equipment from one station point to another station point during the data collection process and installing instruments on a tripod again. In this paper, a case study was conducted using the LiBackpack DGC50 Mobile Scanner, which is the PLS technique, for the cadastral updating surveying in the Karaağaç District of Edirne province. It has been concluded that backpack laser scanners provide sufficient accuracy for cadastral studies in the study area.

Keywords: personnel laser scanners, backpack laser scanner, point clouds, cadastral surveying accuracy, analysis

1. Introduction

Different methods are employed for topography measurements; and generally, aircrafts are preferred when the study site has a coverage field of kilometers. Historically, surveying studies have been performed with theodolites at the beginning, within the more limited distances of the study area. Then, points are enabled to be easily positioned within a global coordinate system with satellite navigation systems. Even though such methods ensure high accuracy and precision for the measurement of points, it requires more time to acquire data with adequate density for digital elevation models (DEMs). Additionally, dense datasets containing millions of point measurements for high-resolution DEMs are now routinely generated using ground-based terrestrial laser scanners (TLSs) with millimeter-centimeter accuracy. After TLSs became ground based, significant developments have occurred in the acquisition of topographic data with mobile laser scanners (MLSs).

MLS has recently been employed to compensate for the shortcomings of TLS. Finally, laser scanners that can be carried or worn by an operator have become popular. These types of scanners are called personal laser scanners (PLS). Depending on how the device is handled, PLS devices are divided into two categories: handheld personal laser scanners (HPLS) and backpack personal laser scanners (BPLSs) [1]. PLS Systems do not need a tripod or tool for use as in TLS, and its most important feature is its high mobility that allows rapid data collection. These systems are capable of digitalizing complex 3D scenarios on the move without a global navigation satellite system (GNSS), thanks to simultaneous localization and mapping (SLAM) algorithms [2, 3] that are based mostly on the robotic operative system [4] for point cloud registration and map extraction [5]. PLS, which are frequently studied in forestry activities, can be utilized in many studies including tree-level data acquisition for forest inventory, measurement of leaf area index of broad fields, and forest route determination for recreation. Laser scanning approaches such as TLS and PLS were employed to collect fuel density data, which bridges the gap between the topography and canopy giving rise to severe canopy fires [6]. On the other hand, data acquired with TLS can require time and include incomplete data and the use of PLS can reduce these drawbacks. For the prediction of tree position and diameter, it was found that the PLS method is faster than TLS about 4.7 times [7]. Also, it is stated that PLS is a very practical and appropriate method to generate the tree inventory and to record different tree characteristics in forested areas where the quality of PLS data matches the necessity of the implementation [8]. It is stated that HPLS is an economical and practical technological solution for data collection, assessment, and processing of individual tree characteristics for forest inventory, generating digital terrain model, harvesting volume computation, and parameterization of forest growth models [9]. Outdoor environment surfaces may be highly uneven, covered with vegetation, and rarely "surround" an observer, and thus represent more tough implementations for reconstruction [10]. It is expected that HPLS will soon become popular in the field of forestry because it could be employed easily in forestry surveys and data could be collected at the required standards [11]. Combining the reliability of laser technique, data density provided specific to scanning systems, the flexibility of walking with a handheld object scanner, and collecting topographic data in complex terrain represent significant advances in laser scanning technology. Generally, HPLS presents significant advantages over existing technologies for the rapid measurement of complex topography with poor field of view and geomorphological study areas. The HPLS system presents high performance considering the enclosed environments where static terrain properties surround the sensor and ensure well-distributed, consistent laser returns to facilitate convergence in the processing algorithms. BPLS combines a single operator while walking when obtaining data with laser scanning technology and inertial measurement units (IMU), a microcomputer, a tablet, and accessories (e.g., connection cables and a battery) in a portable equipment that can be handled. BPLS is a novel type of portable lidar for which the surveyor is the wearable platform, and thus it has a high capacity in terms of accessibility and route choice [12]. The backpack lidar system was designed to automatically collect and register undercopy lidar data [13]. The measurement accuracy and error sources have not been systematically explored for this system [12]. Today, BPLSs are currently used in various fields, from forestry studies [1, 5, 14] to building information model studies

[15]. Compared with TLS, backpack lidar is generally lighter and more portable, and it can obtain much higher quality 3D point clouds in forest with different vegetation structures. In some areas where there is limited access, backpack laser scanning can be integrated with other measurement techniques, especially unmanned aerial vehicles (UAVs) [13].

It is possible to carry out cadastral renewal studies with classical methods. However, if cadastral studies are carried out by establishing a polygon network with classical methods, there are some limitations, such as the requirement that the points in the polygon network see the previous and next ones, the requirement to establish extra points during the work if needed, and the inability to receive signals from a sufficient number of satellites if a polygon is established with GNSS. It is also not possible to obtain the dense point cloud with 3D coordinates provided by the backpack lidar system with classical methods.

In this chapter, the use of a backpack personal laser scanner (BPLS), a PLS system, to update cadastral surveyings is analyzed. For this purpose, accuracy analysis was performed considering the geodetic and lidar measurements. The rest of the chapter is organized as follows: advantages and disadvantages of PLS are specified in section two and the case study section presents a detailed description of the study area and the methodology of the procedures performed. In the conclusion section, it was assessed that backpack laser scanners can be employed to renew property boundaries in places such as the study area.

2. Advantages and disadvantages of personal laser scanners

Collecting the three-dimensional information of objects on earth with high accuracy, and keeping them in the digital environment is a vital task in surveying, object scanning, and mobile mapping. There are multiple ways to obtain three-dimensional information about objects, such as lidar or radar scanning, stereo vision, and imaging sonar. Which of these techniques will be appropriate to employ depends on some parameters such as the size of the study area, expected accuracy, cost, resolution, practicality, and data processing time.

Laser scanning is a surveying method used for mapping topography, vegetation, urban areas and infrastructure, ice, and other targets of interest [16]. According to the platform on which the system is built, laser scanning technology is categorized into airborne, unmanned aircraft systems, terrestrial, mobile, and personal systems [17]. In light of this information, TLS is a ground-based type of lidar built on a tripod. The first studies on the possibilities of applying TLS in laser scanning started around the year 2000. The MLS system, which is an alternative to TLS, is an efficient method since it could decrease occlusion problems and data acquisition time. In addition, appropriate measurement and rapid data collection methods are always preferred [9]. On the other side, MLS systems generally comprise of three primary components: laser scanner (LiDAR sensor), Global Navigation Satellite System (GNSS) receiver, and inertial measurement unit (IMU). The precision and accuracy of all three components and their synchronization affect the accuracy of the MLS data [18]. StreetMapper, which is the first commercial MLS system for surveying implementations, appeared in the market in 2006. Moreover, MLS systems used in surveying and robotics have different perspectives and highlights. The data acquired using the MLS technique is less accurate in comparison to TLS technique due to positioning error propagation in the point cloud produced by MLS. On the other hand, the topographic condition can be not suitable for vehicle motion [9].

To acquire the whole scene with a static scanner, it is necessary to increase the number of scanning stations. One advantage of the PLS compared to the static scanner is that the environment is acquired more easily. Someone can move around the objects of the scene. On the other hand, the PLS data has a lower density of points than the static scanner. Besides a lower point density, the PLS also present a higher measurement noise. The results are very satisfying and promising since the PLS data, which are acquired much faster than TLS data, are close to the reference data. HPLS and BPLS systems provide similar results [15].

The operator's path directly affects the performance of the simultaneous localization and mapping (SLAM) algorithm and the quality of the collected data. Therefore, it should be well-planned and executed. When planning, the time to acquire a point cloud with PLS and cost are factors to consider in measurement planning. PLS point clouds are often georeferenced, as in TLS, by scanning targets of known diameter and location, such as an easy-to-detect and precisely measured sphere, within the point cloud.

The flexibility of the SLAM approach is added to the high accuracy and precision of the TLS systems, making it possible to enrich the final digital model with details undetectable by stationary tools due to the excessive intricacy of the paths [19]. The SLAM algorithm processes IMU and laser data from PLS to locate the scanner in an unknown environment and to register the whole 3D point cloud without the need for GNSS [20]. While rapid changes in sensor technology have led to developments, the most important development in PLS systems is the use of the SLAM algorithm instead of GNSS. The SLAM algorithm processes the IMU and laser data to position the scanner, making it suitable for use in forest-like areas where GNSS signals are absent or weak and distorted. However, current SLAM techniques include remarkable errors. The data acquired by PLS is less precise than TLS point cloud data due to the propagation of positioning errors within PLS point cloud data [21].

3. The case study

This study aims to process laser point data, which is one of the products of backpack laser scanning technology, and to produce the cadastral map using the point cloud. The study area shown in **Figure 1** covers approximately 90 hectares within the borders of Karaağaç District, Edirne province, Türkiye. Karaağaç District has an open space and detached buildings in terms of construction type. In the study area, there is a low-rise construction type, the surroundings of the buildings are relatively open space, and the vegetation is protected (trees, bushes, etc.).

The backpack laser scanner used to obtain point cloud data is LiBackpack DGC50 shown in **Figure 2**. The laser scanning device is a bagged LiBackpack DGC50 device that can produce coordinated and colored point clouds, thanks to the Inertial Navigation System embedded inside. LiFuser-BP Data Processing Software is used.

LiBackpack DGC50 is an operator-only wearable LIDAR 3D scanning system that is suitable for both indoor and outdoor scanning and can produce three-dimensional coordinates with high accuracy. LiBackpack DGC50, which has a panoramic imaging system, produces point cloud data with high accuracy, thanks to GNSS and SLAM technologies. Coordinate information can be obtained even if the GNSS signal is insufficient in some parts of the scanning route. This equipment can be widely employed in indoor and outdoor measurement, obtaining underground information, tunnel engineering, digital mining, counting forestry resource, building information

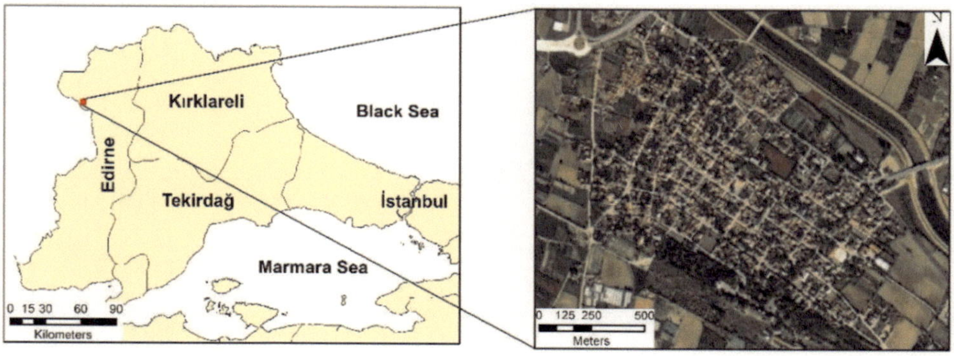

Figure 1.
The location of the study area.

Figure 2.
LiBackpack DGC50 laser scanner.

systems, and other domains. The technical features and parameters of the hardware are shown in **Table 1**.

Before starting data collection, a reconnaissance was made in the study area. According to this, sessions were determined on a 15-minute session-time basis. The total number of sessions in the study area was 63 and the study area scanning was carried out in 7 days. **Figures 3** and **4** show an example of a colored and coordinated point cloud in the study area for a session.

LiBackpack DGC50 provides an output of the point cloud in the form of a raw data file with a ".bag" extension. When the ".mp4" extension video taken simultaneously during scanning is integrated into the point cloud, a point cloud is produced in the real RGB values of the scanned region. In the study, the point cloud obtained on a session basis was processed in the LiFuser-BP program and turned into a point cloud with the ".laz" extension. Then, it was converted into a file with the extension ".las" with the help of cloud compare software. Since the software does not decompress the .laz extension, the conversion process was performed using cloud compare software. The drawing was made using Trimble Business Center (TBC) software.

Point cloud data was produced almost completely and with high accuracy in the selected study area in Karaağaç District. In the scans made in the study area, almost every corner of all the buildings could be drawn. Although it is difficult to distinguish the structures such as coal sheds, sheds, etc. adjacent to the buildings from the main building, the Lidar device's ability to produce point cloud data in color has made it

System	Weight	8.6 kg	GNSS Module	Channels	GPS: L1 C/A, L1C, L2C, L2P, L5. GLONASS: L1, C/A, L2C, L2P, L3, L5 BEIDOU: B1. B2
	Relative Accuracy	3 cm			
	Absolute Accuracy	5–10 cm			
	Power Consumption	50 W		Accuracy	1 cm + 1 ppm
LİDAR	LiDAR Sensors	2	Working Mode		Backpack
	Num of Channels	16 channels	Camera	Resolution	3840*1920
	Scan Range	100 m (20% reflectance)		Frame Rate	30
	FOV (degree)	Vertical($-90 \sim 90$) Horizontal 360		FOV	360
	Scan Rate (single return)	600,000 p/sec		Pixel	18 MP

Table 1.
Specifications of the LiBackpack DGC50 [22].

Figure 3.
Two-dimensional point cloud representation of a session.

easier to detect the separation of the buildings. Since GNSS data could be obtained continuously and uninterruptedly, the scanning process was carried out by producing real-time coordinates. Coordinated point cloud data was produced directly for each session. The point cloud merging process was not performed. The study was conducted on a session basis. After each session was drawn separately, the drawings were combined in the CAD environment. The combined view of the sessions in NetCAD software is given in **Figure 5**.

The study area chosen in Karaağaç District is a region with detached buildings. Since GNSS works at full efficiency, scanning can be done with LiBackpack DGC50

Figure 4.
Three-dimensional point cloud representation of a session.

Figure 5.
The combined view of drawings in the CAD environment.

without establishing any polygons. Polygon points were established with GNSS to measure the coordinates of the detail points determined for accuracy control. The coordinates of 25 detail points were measured from the polygon points with a total station. **Table 2** shows the differences between the classical measurement (with total station) and Lidar measurement for the study area. The maximum difference detected

	Classical Measurement		LIDAR Measurement		Differences	
Point	**Y(m)**	**X (m)**	**Y (m)**	**X (m)**	**ΔY (m)**	**ΔX(m)**
1	460363.829	4613541.392	460363.811	4613541.424	0.018	0.032
2	460363.825	4613534.082	460363.821	4613534.051	0.004	0.031
3	460361.398	4613529.311	460361.422	4613529.302	0.024	0.009
4	460360.993	4613529.671	460361.013	4613529.645	0.020	0.026
5	460360.524	4613536.374	460360.524	4613536.394	0.000	0.020
6	460358.311	4613533.006	460358.325	4613533.062	0.014	0.056
7	460354.802	4613519.903	460354.843	4613519.921	0.041	0.018
8	460352.939	4613548.437	460352.912	4613548.397	0.027	0.040
9	460351.012	4613521.672	460351.044	4613521.643	0.032	0.029
10	460350.601	4613521.911	460350.643	4613521.922	0.042	0.011
11	460347.362	4613540.056	460347.349	4613540.062	0.013	0.006
12	460342.438	4613555.278	460342.391	4613555.311	0.047	0.033
13	460339.626	4613529.059	460339.636	4613529.089	0.010	0.030
14	460339.374	4613550.821	460339.333	4613550.804	0.041	0.017
15	460335.392	4613559.920	460335.334	4613559.911	0.058	0.009
16	460332.393	4613555.384	460332.341	4613555.352	0.052	0.032
17	460332.121	4613492.712	460332.138	4613492.704	0.017	0.008
18	460328.756	4613492.632	460328.772	4613492.621	0.016	0.011
19	460328.519	4613492.776	460328.541	4613492.752	0.022	0.024
20	460322.994	4613483.684	460323.017	4613483.663	0.023	0.021
21	460322.712	4613568.429	460322.691	4613568.415	0.021	0.014
22	460321.538	4613497.288	460321.542	4613497.334	0.004	0.046
23	460317.973	4613473.542	460318.013	4613473.523	0.040	0.019
24	460315.644	4613488.423	460315.702	4613488.409	0.058	0.014
25	460314.301	4613555.951	460314.258	4613555.911	0.043	0.040

Table 2.
Accuracy assessment of the measurements.

is below 7 cm. It has been concluded that the application carried out in the working area with a backpack laser scanner to determine property boundaries remains within the error limits of the regulations. Standard deviation values were calculated with Eq. (1) for X and Y as 0.031 m and 0.025 m, respectively.

$$S = \sqrt{\frac{\sum_{i=1}^{n}(x_i - \hat{x})^2}{n-1}} \quad (1)$$

In eq. (1), n is the number of points, x_i and $\hat{x}$ represent the measured point and arithmetic mean, respectively. Since the study was about determining property boundaries, the accuracy of the Z coordinate was not taken into account.

Parameter	Value
a	−0.0044
b	0.0012
c	0.0008
d	1.0000

Table 3.
Calculated similarity transformation parameters.

For further analysis, the Similarity transformation (Eq. (2)) was applied considering classical measurement reference to the coordinates of each point.

$$\begin{bmatrix} X \\ Y \end{bmatrix} = \lambda R_\alpha \begin{bmatrix} x \\ y \end{bmatrix} + \begin{bmatrix} T_x \\ T_y \end{bmatrix} \qquad (2)$$

In the equation, T_x and T_y represent the shift in the direction of the X and Y axis, R_α represents rotation on the X and Y axis, and λ refers to the scale factor. If equality 1 is explicitly written, the following equation is obtained:

$$X = ax - by + c \qquad (3)$$

$$Y = bx - ay + d \qquad (4)$$

where x and y are the first system coordinates, X and Y are the second system coordinates, and a, b, c, and d are the similarity transformation parameters. Two-dimensional similarity transformation parameters between classical measurements and lidar measurements are given in **Table 3**, and residuals for 25 points are given in **Table 4**. The standard deviation values calculated for the residues are 0.0254 for Y and 0.02 m for X.

4. Conclusion

Backpack laser scanners represent a significant advance in spatial data collection, combining the reliability of laser techniques with the flexibility of measurement. The backpack laser scanning method is faster than the classical method and requires less labor. For the purpose of cadastral renewal studies, a backpack laser scanner, which can produce data at a density equivalent to other scanning systems, was used and evaluated. It was successful in identifying structures such as walls and wires built to determine parcel boundaries. However, it is a fact that the number of noisy data will increase in places with high-rise buildings and narrow streets. Additionally, UAVs can be used to obtain data in areas with limited physical access, such as backyards. In this way, data integration and complete data for the region will be provided.

Listed below are the advantages of backpack laser scanners.

1. In areas with detached and low-rise buildings, BPLS reduces processing steps as they provide coordinate data directly.

2. Scanners that produce colored point clouds provide great convenience to the operator making the drawing in separating the details of complex structures.

Point	V_Y (m)	V_X (m)
1	0.0157	−0.0090
2	−0.0442	0.0051
3	−0.0223	0.0213
4	−0.0319	0.0216
5	0.0084	0.0070
6	0.0402	0.0143
7	0.0131	0.0337
8	−0.0456	−0.0132
9	−0.0338	0.0252
10	0.0065	0.0354
11	−0.0010	0.0001
12	0.0329	−0.0277
13	0.0353	0.0112
14	−0.0146	−0.0212
15	−0.0015	−0.0339
16	−0.0190	−0.0275
17	0.0016	−0.0080
18	0.0043	−0.0181
19	−0.0155	−0.0080
20	−0.0010	−0.0053
21	0.0087	0.0131
22	0.0601	−0.0243
23	0.0031	−0.0034
24	0.0149	0.0286
25	−0.0145	−0.0169

Table 4.
Post-transformation displacements values.

3. Most of the revisions can be made by examining the relevant session without fieldwork again if there is no distortion in the point cloud.

4. Collecting data from the field in the classical method requires more labor. In this respect, BPLS provides flexibility and practicality to the operator during work.

5. Although office work is longer than the classical method, BPLS is more productive when the entire process time is considered.

6. BPLS has some important advantages over TLS and MLS when making field measurements, such as not using a tripod and seeing the object from different directions.

Listed below are the disadvantages of backpack laser scanners.

1. A polygon network should be established before starting measurements in areas where GNSS cannot be used with the desired accuracy in the scanning process.

2. It is affected by limitations such as adjacent buildings and high-rise buildings that make data acquisition difficult.

3. BPLS devices are relatively expensive, so they are not preferred in small-scale fields.

It is clear that as a result of the development of sensor technology in the future, BPLS will find much wider use. Particularly, mobility and speed will make BPLS a practical measurement tool for acquiring three-dimensional data in challenging environments. It has been concluded that backpack laser scanners can be used in the production of cadastral maps in regions such as in this study area.

Acknowledgements

The application data of the study were provided by Halit Enes DEMIR, a Geomatics Engineer who is a master's student of Gebze Technical University.

Conflict of interest

The authors declare no conflict of interest.

Author details

Cumhur Sahin*, Bahadır Ergun and Furkan Bilucan
Gebze Technical University, Kocaeli, Turkey

*Address all correspondence to: csahin@gtu.edu.tr

References

[1] Ko C, Lee S, Yim J, Kim D, Kang J. Comparison of Forest inventory methods at plot-level between a backpack personal laser scanning (BPLS) and conventional equipment in Jeju Island, South Korea. Forests. 2021;**12**(3): 3308. DOI: 10.3390/f12030308

[2] Bailey T, Durrant-Whyte H. Simultaneous localization and mapping (SLAM): Part II. IEEE Robotics & Automation Magazine. 2006;**13**:108-117. DOI: 10.1109/MRA.2006.1678144

[3] Tang J, Chen Y, Chen L, Liu J, Hyyppä J, Kukko A, et al. Fast fingerprint database maintenance for indoor positioning based on UGV SLAM. Sensors. 2015;**15**:5311-5330. DOI: 10.3390/s150305311

[4] Quigley M, Conley K, Gerkey B, Faust J, Foote T, Leibs J. ROS: An open-source robot operating system. In: Proceedings of the ICRA Workshop Open-Source Soft, 17 May 2009, Kobe, Japan. 2019

[5] Cabo C, Del Pozo S, Rodríguez-Gonzálvez P, Ordóñez C, González-Aguilera D. Comparing terrestrial laser scanning (TLS) and wearable laser scanning (WLS) for individual tree modeling at plot level. Remote Sensing. 2018;**10**(4):540. DOI: 10.3390/rs10040540

[6] Forbes B, Reilly S, Clark M, Ferrell R, Kelly A, Krause P, et al. Comparing remote sensing and field-based approaches to estimate ladder fuels and predict wildfire burn severity. Frontiers in Forests and Global Change. 2022;**5**:1-14. DOI: 10.3389/ffgc.2022.818713

[7] Gollob C, Ritter T, Nothdurft A. Forest inventory with long range and high-speed personal laser scanning (PLS) and simultaneous localization and mapping (SLAM) technology. Remote Sensing. 2020;**12**:1509. DOI: 10.3390/rs12091509

[8] Liang X, Kukko A, Kaartinen H, Hyyppä J, Yu X, Jaakkola A, et al. Possibilities of a personal laser scanning system for forest mapping and ecosystem services. Sensors. 2014;**14**: 1228-1248. DOI: 10.3390/s140101228

[9] Chudá J, Hunčaga M, Tuček J, Mokroš M. The handheld mobile laser scanners as a tool for accurate positioning under forest canopy. The International Archives of Photogrammetry, Remote Sensing and Spatial Information Sciences. 2020;**43**: 211-218. DOI: 10.5194/isprs-archives-XLIII-B1-2020-211-202

[10] James MR, Quinton JN. Ultra-rapid topographic surveying for complex environments: The hand-held mobile laser scanner (HMLS). Earth Surface Processes and Landforms. 2014;**39**: 138-142. DOI: 10.1002/esp.3489

[11] Vatandaşlar C, Zeybek M. Application of handheld laser scanning technology for forest inventory purposes in theNE Turkey. Turkish Journal of Agriculture and Forestry. 2020;**44**: 229-242. DOI: 10.3906/tar-1903-40

[12] Xie Y, Zhang J, Chen X, Pang S, Zeng H, Shen Z. Accuracy assessment and error analysis for diameter at breast height measurement of trees obtained using a novel backpack LiDAR system. Forest Ecosystems. 2020;**7**(33):1-11. DOI: 10.1186/s40663-020-00237-0

[13] Su Y, Guan H, Hu T, Guo Q. The integration of uavand backpack LiDAR systems for forest inventory. In:

Proceedings of the IGARSS 2018–2018 IEEE International Geoscience and Remote Sensing Symposium, 22-27 July 2018, Valencia, Spain. 2018. pp. 8757-8760. DOI: 10.1109/IGARSS.2018.8517639

[14] Su Y, Guo Q, Jin S, Guan H, Sun X, Ma Q, et al. The development and evaluation of a backpack LiDAR system for accurate and efficient forest inventory. IEEE Geoscience and Remote Sensing Letters. 2020;**18**(9): 1660-1664. DOI: 10.1109/LGRS.2020.3005166

[15] Salgues H, Macher H, Landes T. Evaluation of mobile mapping systems for indoor surveys. The International Archives of the Photogrammetry, Remote Sensing and Spatial Information Sciences. 2020;**44**:119-125. DOI: 10.5194/isprs-archives-XLIV-4-W1-2020-119-2020

[16] Vasić D, Batilović M, Kuzmić T, Davidović M. The importance of mobile laser scanning in the collection of road infrastructure data. In: FIG Commission 3 Workshop and Annual Meeting 2018 Spatial Information in the Era of Data Science: Challenges and Practical Solutions 3–6 December 2018, Naples, Italy. 2018. pp. 1-13

[17] Balenović I, Liang X, Jurjević L, Hyyppä J, Seletković A, Kukko A. Hand-held personal laser scanning–current status and perspectives for forest inventory application. Croatian Journal of Forest Engineering: Journal for Theory and Application of Forestry Engineering. 2021;**42**:165-183. DOI: 10.5552/crojfe.2021.858

[18] Bauwens S, Bartholomeus H, Calders K, Lejeune P. Forest inventory with terrestrial LiDAR: A comparison of static and hand-held mobile laser scanning. Forests. 2016;**7**:127. DOI: 10.3390/f7060127

[19] Barba S, di Filippo A, Limongiello M, Messina B. Integration of active sensors for geometric analysis of the chapel of the holy shroud. The International Archives of the Photogrammetry, Remote Sensing and Spatial Information Sciences. 2019;**42**:149-156. DOI: 10.5194/isprs-archives-XLII-2-W15-149-2019

[20] Del Perugia B, Giannetti F, Chirici G, Travaglini D. Influence of scan density on the estimation of single-tree attributes by hand-held mobile laser scanning. Forests. 2019;**10**(3):277. DOI: 10.3390/f10030277

[21] Chen S, Liu H, Feng Z, Shen C, Chen P. Applicability of personal laser scanning in forestry inventory. PLoS One. 2019;**14**(2):e0211392. DOI: 10.1371/journal.pone.0211392

[22] GreenValley International. LiBackpack DGC50. Available from: https://greenvalleyintl.com/static/upload/file/20220628/1656388497142715.pdf [Accessed: November 28, 2023]

Chapter 2

Novel Approaches for Point Cloud Analysis with Evidential Methods: A Multifaceted Approach to Object Pose Estimation, Point Cloud Odometry, and Sensor Registration

Vedant Bhandari, Tyson Phillips and Ross McAree

Abstract

Autonomous agents must understand their environment to make decisions. Perception systems often interpret point cloud measurements to extract beliefs about their surroundings. A common strategy is to seek beliefs that are least likely to be false, commonly known as cost-based approaches. These metrics have limitations in practical applications, such as in the presence of noisy measurements, dynamic objects, and debris. Modern solutions integrate additional stages such as segmentation to counteract these limitations, thereby increasing the complexity of the algorithms while being internally flawed. An alternative strategy is to extract beliefs that are best supported by the data. We call these evidence-based methods. This difference allows for robustness to the limitations of using cost-based methods without needing complex additional stages. Essential perception tasks such as object pose estimation, point cloud odometry, and sensor registration are solved using evidence-based methods. The demonstrated approaches are simple, require minimum configuration and tuning, and circumvents the need for additional processing stages.

Keywords: evidential, point cloud, pose estimation, sensor registration, point cloud odometry

1. Introduction

A fundamental capability for robotic agents is the capacity to perceive the environment in which they operate. This capability is often achieved via the interpretation of point cloud measurements provided by onboard sensors such as Light Detection And Ranging (LiDAR). The established beliefs must be robust, accurate and time-bounded, as they are used to inform control actions.

A popularized strategy for extracting beliefs from point cloud measurements is to fit data to a hypothesis, that is, accepting the hypothesis that best validates the data. We call these strategies 'cost-based methods', e.g. the Iterative Closest Point (ICP)

method [1, 2]. A fundamentally different strategy is to fit the hypothesis to the data, that is, accepting the hypothesis that would most likely reproduce the data. We call these strategies 'evidence-based methods', e.g. the Normal Distributions Transform (NDT) method [3].

At a surface level, it may seem that these strategies are the same thing worded differently, however, the two approaches yield very different solutions, with the latter being much more robust to challenges arising in real-world applications. In non-segmented data, any hypothesized belief will appear improbable of reproducing the complete measurement set. Our proposed evidence-based strategies accept improbable beliefs so long as they are the most probable. As Sherlock Holmes suggests [4], "... and improbable as it is, all other explanations are more improbable still."

This chapter demonstrates how Evidence-based methods can be used to address three common perception problems that arise in the interpretation of point cloud measurements. These are:

1. *Object pose estimation*: Robotic agents often need to find and interact with known geometries in their environment. This problem involves estimating the pose, $\hat{\mathbf{T}}_{\mathcal{S}\to\mathcal{M}}$, of a known geometry model described in a model-fixed frame, $\mathcal{M}$, relative to a sensor (or other) coordinate frame, $\mathcal{S}$ (see **Figure 1a**).

2. *Point cloud odometry*: This problem arises whereby a robotic agent needs to know it's location within an established map. We formulate this as finding the pose, $\hat{\mathbf{T}}_{\mathcal{M}\to\mathcal{S}}$, that best fits a new point cloud, $\mathbf{Z}_{\mathcal{S}}$, to an existing point cloud map, $\mathbf{Z}_{\mathcal{M}}$ (see **Figure 1b**).

3. *Sensor registration*: Extrinsic calibration, or sensor registration, involves estimating a sensor's pose, $\hat{\mathbf{T}}_{\mathcal{P}\to\mathcal{S}}$, relative to a platform coordinate frame, $\mathcal{P}$. We provide a method that seeks to provide consistency between m scans, $\mathbf{Z}_{\mathcal{S}_{1:m}}$, taken from m platform poses, $\mathbf{T}_{\mathcal{W}\to\mathcal{P}_{1:m}}$, that are known within a World coordinate frame, $\mathcal{W}$ (see **Figure 1c**).

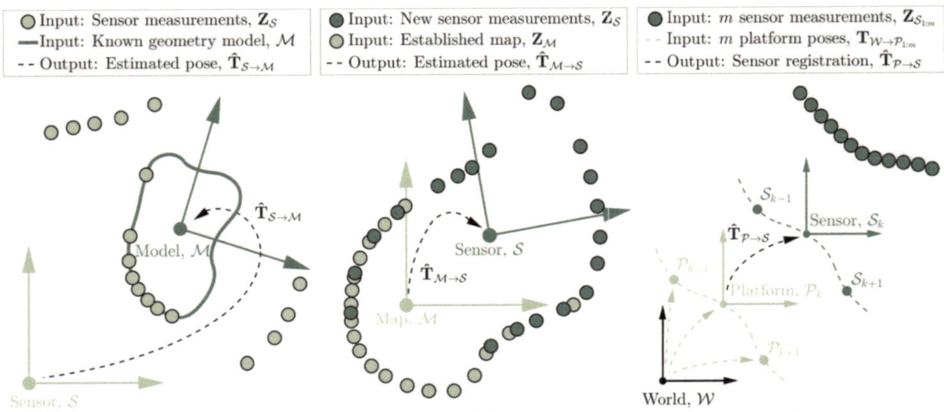

Figure 1.
This chapter demonstrates evidential methods towards three candidate problems that commonly arise in the interpretation of point cloud measurements. Namely, the estimation of: (a) an object's pose, $\hat{\mathbf{T}}_{\mathcal{S}\to\mathcal{M}}$, within a point cloud; (b) a platform or sensor's location, $\hat{\mathbf{T}}_{\mathcal{M}\to\mathcal{S}}$, within a map; and (c) a sensor's installed pose, $\hat{\mathbf{T}}_{\mathcal{P}\to\mathcal{S}}$, aboard a moving platform.

This chapter explores the transformative potential of using evidential methods in point cloud analysis. Section 2 explores the state-of-the art where cost and evidence approaches are employed. Several challenges that occur in extracting beliefs from point cloud data are presented in Section 3. Particular attention is shown as to why these challenges present predictable failure modes to cost-based methods but do not inhibit evidence-based methods. Section 4 demonstrates how evidence is established from point cloud data to support hypotheses about the environment. The use of evidential methods are then demonstrated against the three candidate problems of pose estimation, localization, and sensor registration in Sections 5-7. Concluding remarks are made in Section 8.

2. Background and introduction to relevant literature

This section introduces the idea behind cost and evidence-based metrics, followed by exploring existing approaches to solving the three problems introduced previously, using cost, evidence, and learning-based approaches.

2.1 Commonalities in the three perception problems

The object pose estimation, localization and mapping, and sensor registration problems involve matching or aligning two inputs to estimate a homogeneous transform. We denote the two inputs as a source and reference, as is commonly used in existing literature. For the object pose estimation problem, the source is a point cloud and the reference is a known geometry, with the task of locating the known geometry in the point cloud. The geometry may be represented as a triangulated mesh or a sampled point cloud of the mesh. For the localization problem, both the source and reference are point clouds, used to estimate the transform of the sensor between both point clouds. The sensor registration problem is slightly different in that it aims to find the rigid transform between the sensor and the platform frame. Still, it aims to accurately align a series of point clouds to uncover the unknown transform.

2.2 Cost-based vs. evidence-based metrics

Approaches to solving these problems generally follow a similar structure consisting of two main components – (1) an objective function that provides a quantitative metric to differentiate pose hypotheses, whether this be the pose or configuration of an object in a point cloud, the pose between two point clouds, or the pose from the platform to the sensor used to align scans, and, (2) a search algorithm used to find the hypothesis that provides the best result from the objective function. Here, we focus on the first component, the objective function.

Figure 2 illustrates a simple example of an object pose estimation to introduce and highlight the distinction between cost and evidence-based approaches. Cost-based approaches penalize scan points for being located further away from the source. **Figure 2a** shows the cost map for a known geometry in a hypothesized pose, $\hat{\mathbf{T}}_{\mathcal{S}\rightarrow\mathcal{M}}$. Scan points close to the geometry incur a low cost, whereas points located further away have a higher cost. This is intuitive in that corresponding points in the scan and model will obtain zero error if they are closely aligned and a large error otherwise. This assumption only holds if all points correspond to the model, i.e. the point cloud is segmented. **Figure 2c**, shows the resulting estimate of a cost-based metric in a

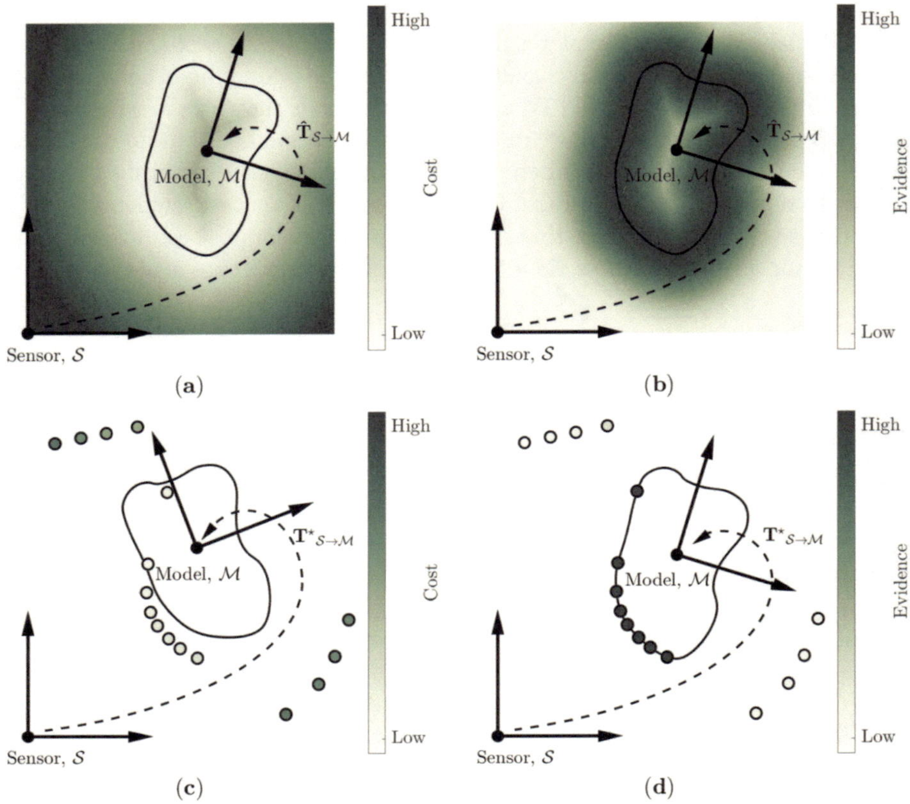

Figure 2.
An object pose estimation problem used to illustrate the distinction between cost and evidence-based metrics. A cost map of a known geometry, $\mathcal{M}$, is shown in (a), where points located near the surface incur zero error, with the cost increasing away from the surface. Non-model points detract from the true pose leading to misalignment. The minimum cost solution, $\mathbf{T}^{\star}{}_{\mathcal{S}\to\mathcal{M}}$, is shown in (c). The evidence-based metric, shown in (b), overcomes this limitation as points located near the surface contribute high evidence whereas points located further from the surface do not contribute any evidence. The maximum evidence solution, $\mathbf{T}^{\star}{}_{\mathcal{S}\to\mathcal{M}}$, is shown is shown in (d).

non-segmented point cloud. Locating the geometry with the true solution is unfavourable by the cost metric as the non-model points incur a high cost. This problem is overcome by using an evidence-based metric where there is no consequence for having non-model points in the scene. **Figure 2b** displays the evidence map for the same geometry located via the same estimate. Scan points located close to the geometry provide high evidence, whereas points located further from the geometry provide no evidence. This allows for accurate alignment as shown in **Figure 2d**. The difference allows for a robust foundation for solving the three problems explored in this chapter.

2.3 Cost-based approaches

The most common and prominent example of a cost-based approach is the Iterative Closest Point (ICP) algorithm proposed by Chen and Medioni [2] and Besl and McKay [1]. ICP introduced a simple and efficient method for solving object pose estimation and scan alignment problems, predicated on the belief that the best alignment between two scans or a scan and a geometry is given when the point-to-point distance between the reference and source is minimized. Mathematically, ICP aims to find the homogeneous transform, $\hat{\mathbf{T}}^{\star}_{\mathcal{S}\to\mathcal{M}}$, that minimizes point-to-point/point-to-model distances when applied to the scan, $\mathbf{Z}_{\mathcal{S}}$,

$$\mathbf{T}^{\star}_{\mathcal{S}\to\mathcal{M}} = \arg\min_{j} \left\{ \sum_{i=1}^{n} \| z_{i|j} - r_k \| \right\}, \tag{1}$$

where $z_{i|j}$ is the i-th point of the scan located by the j-th hypothesis, $\hat{\mathbf{T}}_{\mathcal{S}\to\mathcal{M},j}$, and where r_k is the closest reference point to $z_{i|j}$. ICP is independent of shape representation and normally distributed noise, however, the application finds significant limitations when used with real-world data. Nevertheless, the past 30 years have seen the rising application of ICP as the foundation for many algorithms with an increasing number of additional stages to overcome its limitations. For example, Sun et al. [5] use fast point feature histograms to decrease ICP's sensitivity to the initial guess, Yu et al. [6] introduce pre-processing filters to denoise the scans to achieve a more accurate alignment, and Zhang et al. [7] propose pose search efficiencies to achieve real-time performance. Donoso et al. [8] explore the performance of 20,637 variants of ICP for scan matching terrain point clouds and find that no single variant satisfies all criteria. They proceed to propose three new variants to meet the required performance [9]. Pomerleau et al. [10] and Rusinkiewicz and Levoy [11] illustrate the recursive spawning of variants to tailor the ICP implementation to the application, increasing the complexity and failure mechanisms of the algorithm.

2.4 Evidence-based approaches

Evidence-based approaches model the problem as a maximum likelihood estimation problem. These methods claim to overcome many of the core limitations of ICP while improving the accuracy and timeliness of solutions. Two prominent approaches include the Coherent Point Drift (CPD) method by Myronenko and Song [12] and the Normal Distributions Transform (NDT) by Biber and Strasser [3]. CPD handles both rigid and non-rigid point cloud-to-point cloud matching by representing each set of points as a Gaussian Mixture Model and searching for the transform that maximizes the likelihood when the two sets are aligned. The approach demonstrates state-of-the-art performance in noisy and cluttered environments, however, it is computationally expensive. NDT aims to find the homogeneous transform, $\mathbf{T}^{\star}_{\mathcal{S}\to\mathcal{M}}$, that maximizes per point likelihood,

$$\mathbf{T}^{\star}_{\mathcal{S}\to\mathcal{M}} = \arg\max_{j} \left\{ \sum_{i=1}^{n} \exp\left(\frac{-\left(z_{i|j} - q_i\right)^{t} \Sigma_i^{-1} \left(z_{i|j} - q_i\right)}{2} \right) \right\}. \tag{2}$$

where, q_i and Σ_i correspond to the local mean and covariance for $z_{i|j}$ respectively. The distinction between cost and evidence-based metrics is evident by comparing Eqs. (1) and (2). NDT provides robustness to noise and clutter, however, it is sensitive to a grid size parameter used to establish local distributions [13]. The authors note that the selection of the grid size parameter depends on the shape of the input data and its application [14].

2.5 Learning-based approaches

Recently, deep learning frameworks have been integrated with fine registration methods such as ICP and NDT to provide faster convergence without the requirement of a good initial pose. Ahmdali et al. [15] use deep learning to match features in the source and reference to decrease computation time and provide a coarse guess for the finer registration process using ICP. The solution provides improved performance with significant occlusions and minimal overlap. Wang and Solomon [16] demonstrate state-of-the-art performance with Deep Closest Point. Their proposed pipeline uses a Dynamic Graph CNN and an attention module to extract correspondences required to estimate the rigid transform between the source and reference. However, there are two main disadvantages of learning-based approaches that limit their usability in applications requiring functionally safe performance. Firstly, the performance relies on having sufficient training data for accurate performance, and secondly, understanding failure mechanisms is difficult with errors not always being traceable through the many layers in a deep-learning network. Ideally, a deterministic and traceable algorithm is required to allow failure modes to be understood and accounted for.

3. Challenges in extracting beliefs from point clouds

Point clouds provide no semantic information about the environment they represent. Extracting beliefs from point cloud data requires interpretation, a process that is challenged by numerous mechanisms, some of which are explored in this section.

3.1 Point clouds contain measurement uncertainty

Several sources of uncertainty are inherent to the measurement process of point cloud sensors. Perception sensors such as LiDAR have documented range measurement uncertainty. There is also uncertainty in the per-beam intrinsic calibration used to describe the elevation and heading of the range measurement [17, 18]. Point cloud measurements are often interpreted in a different coordinate system to the sensor frame. This requires accurate extrinsic calibration (sensor registration) to determine the relative pose between the platform and sensor [19, 20]. It is not reasonable to expect a zero-cost pose solution in light of these sources of measurement uncertainty.

3.2 Point clouds do not arrive with perfect correspondence

Cost-based methods assume correspondence, that is, they assume all source measurements belong to the reference model. This assumption is rarely valid. **Figure 3a** displays two successive scans captured by a vehicle travelling on a highway. Attempting to match these scans is problematic as not all measurements should appear in both scans. This is because (i) dynamic objects will have moved between scans, and (ii) the new scan will observe a different part of the environment compared to the previous scan. The use of an evidence-based metric alleviates this problem as non-corresponding points do not detract from the true pose being accepted.

3.3 Point cloud sensors are susceptible to environmental conditions

Atmospheric obscurants such as dust and fog inhibit the capacity of perception sensors to provide an accurate representation of the environment [22]. **Figure 3b** shows a scan captured during an excavator's loading cycle. A large amount of dust is disturbed, presenting as spurious measurements in the point cloud (dark green).

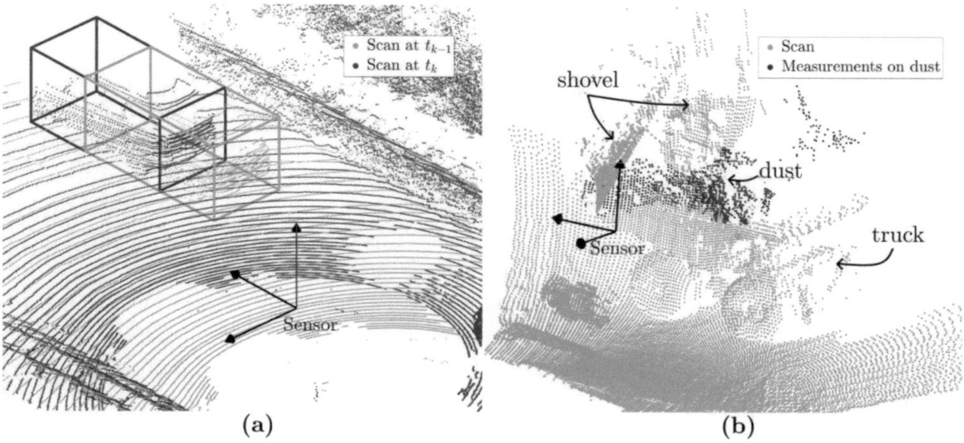

Figure 3.
Two key challenges involve extracting beliefs in the presence of dynamic objects and debris. Two successive scans captured onboard a moving vehicle from the KITTI dataset [21] are displayed in (a). Aligning the scans using the relative pose estimate reveals a moving vehicle in the environment. The presence of such dynamic objects corrupts the assumption of static point cloud used for point cloud-to-point cloud matching. A scan captured from a LiDAR mounted to a rope shovel is shown in (b). Dust occludes the view of the shovel's dipper and the truck.

Consider the problem of estimating the pose of a haul truck model in the point cloud data. The measurements attributed to dust would inhibit a cost-based metric as they do not correspond to the model and are challenging to automatically segment. An evidence metric would find that these spurious measurements do not support the true pose of the truck, however, they do not detract from the true pose being accepted, hence bypassing the need to segment measurements attributed to atmospheric obscurants.

3.4 Real-time point cloud processing is challenging

It is challenging to extract beliefs in real time from high-density point cloud measurements. Point clouds generated by common sensors such as the Ouster OS1-64 provide up to 2,621,440 points per second [23]. Interpreting point clouds of this size presents a bottleneck for most algorithms. Reducing the number of points by subsampling the data using radial or voxel-based approaches allows for faster processing at the cost of reduced information about the scene. Due to the lack of semantic information, algorithms often require multiple pre-processing filters to clean the scan before use. For example, several algorithms perform ground plane fitting [24] to identify and segment ground points and use the remaining point cloud for interpretation. In the sections that follow, we provide computationally efficient approximations of evidence that enable real-time interpretation.

4. Evidential methods in point cloud analysis

This section introduces the concept of evidential methods in point cloud analysis. It explores the notion of ray-based evidential analysis, including the construction of a per-point "evidential" and the principle of Maximum Sum of Evidentials. These ideas are originally presented in [25].

4.1 How does a point provide evidence towards a hypothesis?

Evidential methods are predicated on the belief that the likelihood of an estimate is correlated with the likelihood of reproducing the observed measurements. The likelihood of reproducing point cloud measurements can be ascertained via a sensor measurement model. Here, we consider the measurement model of a range-scanning LiDAR sensor. A LiDAR sensor produces range measurements over a set of beam heading and elevation angles. The expected range measurements are obtained by raycasting against a hypothesized environment, **H**. **Figure 4a** depicts the raycasting operation performed along the i-th beam against the j-th environment hypothesis, $\mathbf{H_j}$. The raycasted range measurement, $\hat{z}_{i|j}$, is directly comparable to the observed measurement, z_i, along the same beam. In this case, it is shown to be a slightly longer range.

The observed measurement, z_i, provides a measure of evidential support for the hypothesis, $\mathbf{H}_j$. This support is quantified via a conditional range likelihood model, $f(z_i|\mathbf{H}_j)$, describing the likelihood of obtaining measurement z_i conditional to the hypothesis $\mathbf{H}_j$ being assumed. This probability density function is established by considering sources of uncertainty in the measuring process of the LiDAR. A simple uncertainty model is to consider the range accuracy of the sensor itself. The measurement uncertainty can be modelled as having a standard deviation, σ, which is typically in the order of several centimetres. **Figure 4b** depicts the measurement likelihood model overlayed on the i-th beam, calculated as,

$$f(z_i|\mathbf{H}_j) = \mathcal{N}(z_i|\hat{z}_{i|j}, \sigma^2) = \frac{1}{\sqrt{2\pi\sigma^2}} \exp\left(-\frac{(z_i - \hat{z}_{i|j})^2}{2\sigma^2}\right). \quad (3)$$

The measurement likelihood model, $f(z_i|\mathbf{H}_j)$, can be extended to include any source of uncertainty in the measuring process (e.g. those sources of measurement uncertainty discussed in Section 3.1). For example, uncertainty in the sensor's pose could result in a beam intersecting different locations of the hypothesized environment. We explore these ideas further in [25] where uncertainties (such as intrinsic

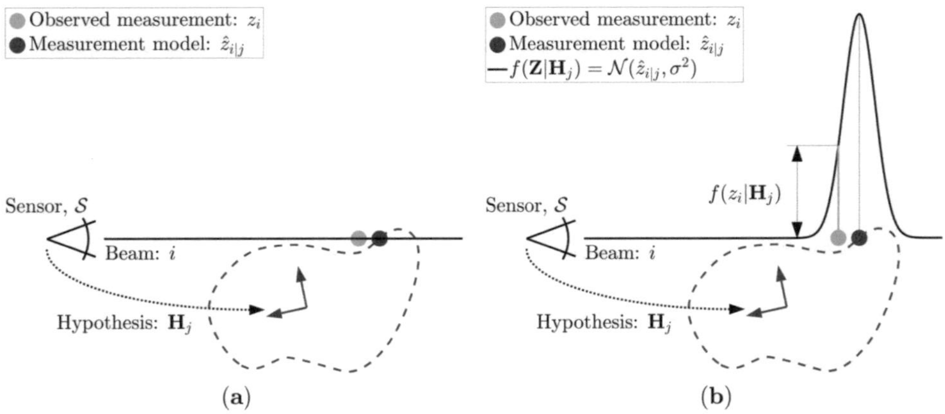

Figure 4.
(a) A geometry model is located with an assumed Hypothesis, $\mathbf{H}_j$. Under this hypothesis, the measurement $\hat{z}_{i|j}$ would be observed along the i-th beam. (b) The likelihood of observing z_i conditional to the hypothesis $\mathbf{H}_j$ is modelled as $f(z_i|\mathbf{H}_j)$ using the sensor's range uncertainty σ. Figure from Ref. [25].

and extrinsic calibration) are mapped to range likelihood via sampling techniques. However, for most of our work, we have found that the simple model of range uncertainty is sufficient.

4.2 How do we find the hypothesis with the most evidence?

Having established how to evaluate per-point evidence towards a hypothesis, we now seek to determine the hypothesis with the most evidence, $\mathbf{H}^{\star}$. We illustrate this problem using the point cloud of $N = 9$ range measurements shown in **Figure 5a**. Here, a robot is parameterized by a two-dimensional hypothesis, $\mathbf{H}_j = [\theta_{1,j}, \theta_{2,j}]^T$.

A brute force approach sums the evidence for all measurements at a finely discretized set of robot configurations across the entire workspace. Doing so produces the surface shown in **Figure 5b**. A global maximum of evidence is indicated at $\mathbf{H}^{\star} = [28.6^{\circ}, 114.6^{\circ}]$, which also corresponds to the true pose depicted in **Figure 5a**. This is the basis of evidential point cloud analysis, the hypothesis with the most per-point evidence is the most likely to be true. An alternate hypothesis, indicated by $\mathbf{H}_A$, is shown to produce a local maximum of evidence. **Figure 5c** shows the robot

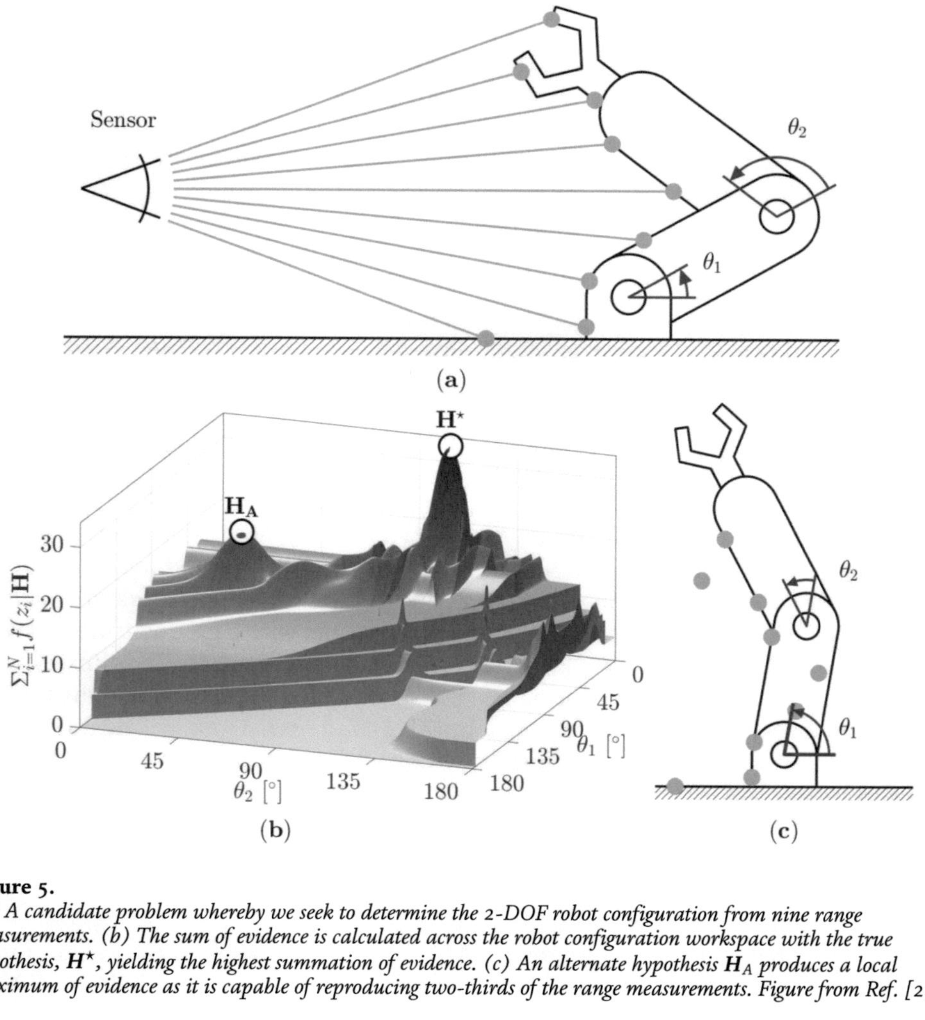

Figure 5.
(a) A candidate problem whereby we seek to determine the 2-DOF robot configuration from nine range measurements. (b) The sum of evidence is calculated across the robot configuration workspace with the true hypothesis, $\mathbf{H}^{\star}$, yielding the highest summation of evidence. (c) An alternate hypothesis $\mathbf{H}_A$ produces a local maximum of evidence as it is capable of reproducing two-thirds of the range measurements. Figure from Ref. [25].

articulated with hypothesis $\mathbf{H}_A$. It can be seen that this pose is capable of reproducing six of the nine range measurements. Accordingly, this hypothesis garners two-thirds of the evidence produced by the true solution, $\mathbf{H}^\star$. Increasing the density of measurements further separates the disparity of evidence between $\mathbf{H}^\star$ and $\mathbf{H}_A$.

4.3 What are the limitations of evidential methods?

The brute force approach presented in the previous section is not a viable approach for time-bounded applications. Raycasting against hypothesized environments is a computationally expensive operation. The number of raycasting operations is proportional to both the number of range measurements and the number of hypotheses tested. It is possible to pre-calculate raycast measurements for a discretized set of hypotheses over a bounded hypothesis space. These precalculated tables of raycast values can then be used to evaluate observed range measurements as they arrive. However, the number of precalculated raycasts quickly increases with the dimensionality of the hypothesis space, making this approach impractical for larger hypothesis spaces.

In the candidate applications that follow, we present the concept of Evidential Rapid Approximation (ERA), a method designed to streamline the computation of evidentials, making the process more viable for real-time applications. For pose estimation (Section 5), we approximate the range likelihood by considering the proximity of point cloud measurements to the surface of a known geometry at a hypothesized pose. Similarly, for localization and mapping (Section 6), evidence is determined by the proximity of new point cloud measurements relative to previously mapped points. Both strategies are an approximation of evidence, neither of which requires the computationally expensive raycasting operation.

5. Applications for object pose estimation – PLuM

The Pose Lookup Method (PLuM) is detailed in Ref. [26] and summarized here.

5.1 Problem overview and applications

The object pose estimation task involves estimating the pose, $\hat{\mathbf{T}}_{\mathcal{S}\to\mathcal{M}}$, of a known geometry described in frame, $\mathcal{M}$, within a point cloud, $\mathbf{Z}_{\mathcal{S}}$, captured in the sensor (or other) frame, $\mathcal{S}$. This task is encountered in diverse applications. For example, digital quality inspection matches scans of physical components with a ground truth model to highlight manufacturing defects [27], removing the dependence on Coordinate-Measuring Machines. The bioinformatics industry requires similar algorithms for various tasks such as protein surface matching [28] and retinal image registration [29]. A large area of research is dedicated to body pose estimation dealing with both rigid and deformable models of humans [30], with an application in identifying pedestrians from autonomous vehicles for safer navigation. Numerous use-cases also arise in the automation of mining and agricultural equipment, with the use of object pose estimation for end-effector tracking [31], and identifying known geometries in the workspace from haul trucks [32] to peach trees [33].

The Pose Lookup Method [26], or PLuM, is an approximation of the Maximum Sum of Evidence method described in the previous section that is grounded in ERA.

PLuM provides a real-time and accurate method for the 6-DOF pose estimation of known geometries in point cloud data, with extensions to kinematic configuration spaces such as estimating the joint angles for an articulated robot similar to the example displayed in **Figure 5**. For this application, the source is a point cloud and the reference is a model of the geometry as depicted in **Figure 1a**, with the objective of finding the ideal transform, $\mathbf{T}^{\star}_{\mathcal{S}\to\mathcal{M}}$, that best fits the model to the point cloud data.

5.2 PLuM formulation

PLuM evaluates the per-point evidence using an approximation of Eq. (3), where the difference between the measurement and the raycast measurement, $\left(z_i - \hat{z}_{i|j}\right)$, is replaced with the closest distance, $d_{i|j}$, between the reference point, $p_{\mathcal{S},i}$, and the model as depicted in **Figure 6**. The evidence, $e_{i|j}$, for point, $p_{\mathcal{S},i}$, is given by a zero-mean Gaussian function,

$$e_{i|j} = \mathcal{N}\left(d_{i|j}|0,\sigma^2\right) = \frac{1}{\sqrt{2\pi\sigma^2}}\exp\left(-\frac{d_{i|j}^2}{2\sigma^2}\right). \tag{4}$$

The evidence is calculated with the user-selected configuration parameter, σ. The evidence value is at a maximum when the point cloud measurement lies on the surface of the model, corresponding to $d_{i|j} = 0$, and decreases as the distance between the point cloud measurement and the model increases. As the evidence value is used as a comparative measure between pose hypotheses, the normalisation factor, $\frac{1}{\sqrt{2\pi\sigma^2}}$, can be discarded,

$$e_{i|j} = \exp\left(-\frac{d_{i|j}^2}{2\sigma^2}\right). \tag{5}$$

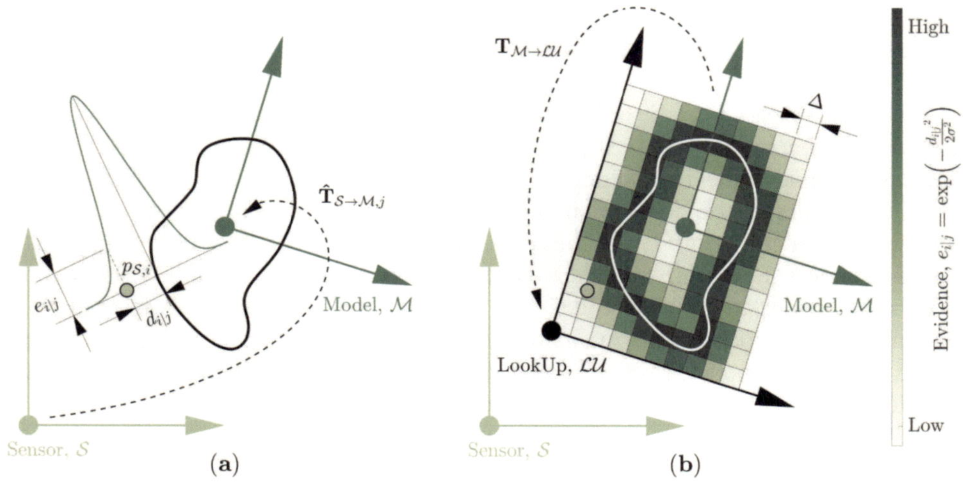

Figure 6.
(a) PLuM computes the evidence, $e_{i|j}$, using a zero-mean Gaussian evaluation of the closest distance between the source point, $p_{\mathcal{S},i}$, and the model, $\mathcal{M}$. (b) A lookup frame, $\mathcal{LU}$, is rigidly fixed to the model, $\mathcal{M}$, and allows for a direct lookup of evidence for point cloud measurements near the model's surface. Figure from Ref. [26].

A major factor inhibiting real-time applicability is the expensive calculation of point-to-model distances, $d_{i|j}$, used for the evidence calculation in Eq. (5). PLuM overcomes this limitation by using a pre-computed lookup table of point-to-model distances. **Figure 6** depicts the problem and the application of a lookup table used for the evidence calculation. A lookup frame, $\mathcal{LU}$, is rigidly attached to the geometry to capture a bounding region of pixels (or voxels in 3D) around it. The region is discretized at some resolution, Δ, with each pixel encoding the closest distance to the geometry. The evidence calculation is performed by the following three steps.

1. The frame transform between the lookup and the sensor frame, $\hat{\mathbf{T}}_{\mathcal{LU}\to\mathcal{S}|j}$, is calculated using the j-th pose hypothesis, $\hat{\mathbf{T}}_{\mathcal{S}\to\mathcal{M},j}$, and the known rigid transform from the model to the lookup table, $\mathbf{T}_{\mathcal{M}\to\mathcal{LU}}$,

$$\hat{\mathbf{T}}_{\mathcal{LU}\to\mathcal{S}|j} = \left(\hat{\mathbf{T}}_{\mathcal{S}\to\mathcal{M},j}\mathbf{T}_{\mathcal{M}\to\mathcal{LU}}\right)^{-1}. \tag{6}$$

2. The i-th point in the source point cloud frame, $p_{\mathcal{S},i}$, is calculated in the lookup frame as,

$$p_{\mathcal{LU},i} = \hat{\mathbf{T}}_{\mathcal{LU}\to\mathcal{S}|j}\, p_{\mathcal{S},i} = \begin{bmatrix} x_i \\ y_i \\ z_i \\ 1 \end{bmatrix}_{\mathcal{LU}}. \tag{7}$$

3. The x_i, y_i, and z_i values are used to index the pre-calculated distances stored in the lookup table,

$$d_{i|j} = \text{lookup}\left(\lfloor\frac{x_{i,\mathcal{LU}}}{\Delta}\rfloor, \lfloor\frac{y_{i,\mathcal{LU}}}{\Delta}\rfloor, \lfloor\frac{z_{i,\mathcal{LU}}}{\Delta}\rfloor\right), \tag{8}$$

where $\lfloor . \rfloor$ is the floor function and Δ is the lookup table resolution.

5.3 Example point cloud-to-model matching

The evidence-based metric offers robustness to clutter, with the use of lookup tables offering a significant increase in speed. A sample result for estimating the 6-DOF pose of a Stanford dragon model to a point cloud with 90% clutter is shown in **Figure 7**. Similar behaviour to the scenario depicted in **Figure 2** is visible, with the ICP solution corrupted due to the presence of clutter, and the evidence-based approach only rewarding points that best support the hypothesis. The 6-DOF pose hypotheses are listed in **Table 1**.

PLuM provides an accurate and timely approach to answering the 'where is it?' question. Open problems remain about identifying the presence of multiple models or the absence of the model from the scene, as the approach described above will always provide an estimate of the model in the scene.

6. Applications for point cloud odometry – SiMpLE

The Simple Mapping and Localisation Estimation (SiMpLE) algorithm is detailed in [34] and summarized here.

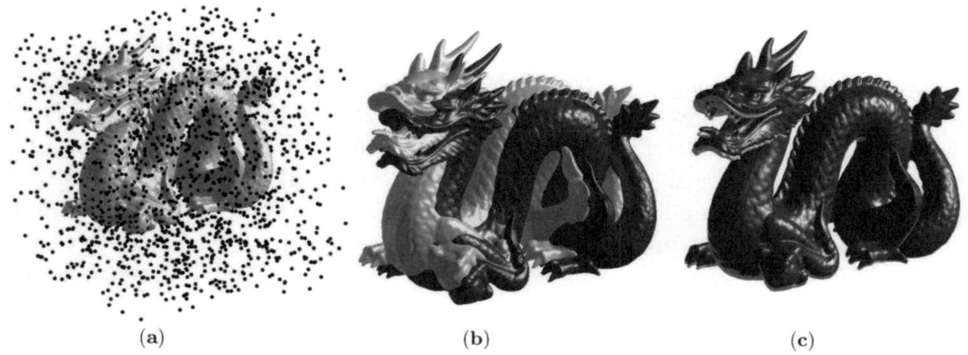

Figure 7.
A demonstration of using cost-based vs. evidence-based metrics for object pose estimation. The problem is depicted in (a), with a point cloud consisting of 90% clutter and a dragon model located in its true pose (light green model). Vanilla ICP fails to align the dragon's pose (dark green model in (b)), whereas PLuM accurately aligns the model with the point cloud (dark green model in (c)).

Source	roll [deg]	pitch [deg]	yaw [deg]	x [mm]	y [mm]	z [mm]
True pose	90.000	0.000	0.000	0.180	0.160	0.000
Vanilla ICP	93.011	−2.123	−6.075	0.192	0.155	−0.007
PLuM	89.487	0.785	0.317	0.178	0.157	0.002

Table 1.
The object pose estimation results using Vanilla ICP and PLuM. PLuM provides a significantly better fit compared to ICP.

6.1 Problem overview

Point cloud odometry is an approach used to localize an autonomous agent within an environment. Successive scans are matched to recover the change in the sensor's pose as depicted in **Figure 1b**. Sequential computation of relative poses allows for recursive pose estimation, whereby the pose at time t_k is based on the point cloud at time t_k, the previous pose estimate at time t_{k-1}, and some history of the previous scans. This is commonly known as the front-end for Simultaneous Localization and Mapping (SLAM) algorithms. Due to the dead-reckoning behaviour, the approach is prone to drift over long sequences with the accumulation of errors. A back-end is typically employed to optimize pose estimates using loop closure constraints. A low-drift front-end is desired for accurate pose estimation and to aid the back-end computation.

Point cloud-to-point cloud matching is based on the assumption of observing similar features in both scans that can be matched to recover the change in the sensor's pose. This assumes a static environment as features must be consistent to allow for correct matching. However, agents such as autonomous vehicles operate in highly dynamic environments with the presence of pedestrians and other vehicles. The challenges associated with using cost-based metrics discussed in Section 3 arise. Dynamic points corrupting the scan matching process and partial overlap in scans from a moving platform invalidate the assumption of direct correspondence.

6.2 Existing approaches

Existing scan-matching approaches are often augmented with additional stages to overcome these challenges. For example, many approaches such as LOAM [35] and F-LOAM [16] extract geometric features such as lines and planes between scans to aid the scan matching process. MULLS [24] extend this to identifying environment-specific features such as pillars and beams while continuing to utilize ICP at their core for fine registration. Alternative methods augment deep-learning networks to help with feature extraction and dynamic object detection [36–38]. While these additional stages improve performance, they also increase complexity and the associated burden of configuration. Ideally, a low configuration and accurate odometry solution is required for use-case agnostic applications among various types of sensors and environments.

SiMpLE has the advantage of providing accurate localization in various applications while having a minimum configuration set consisting of only five parameters. In comparison, most existing approaches have a significant configuration burden. For example, CT-ICP [39] has 30 parameters, SuMa [40] has 49 parameters, and MULLS has 107 parameters. Methods such as LOAM and MULLS rely heavily on feature extraction to aid the registration process. This requires significantly more tuning, and the results are sensitive to the application environment. A practical disadvantage of using SiMpLE and similar methods is the requirement of multithreading to achieve real-time performance, as discussed in Section 3.4.

6.3 SiMpLE formulation

Here, we introduce Simple Mapping and Localization Estimation, or SiMpLE [34]. This scan-to-map registration algorithm seeks to maximize per-point evidence, overcoming many limitations associated with classical scan matching algorithms. The

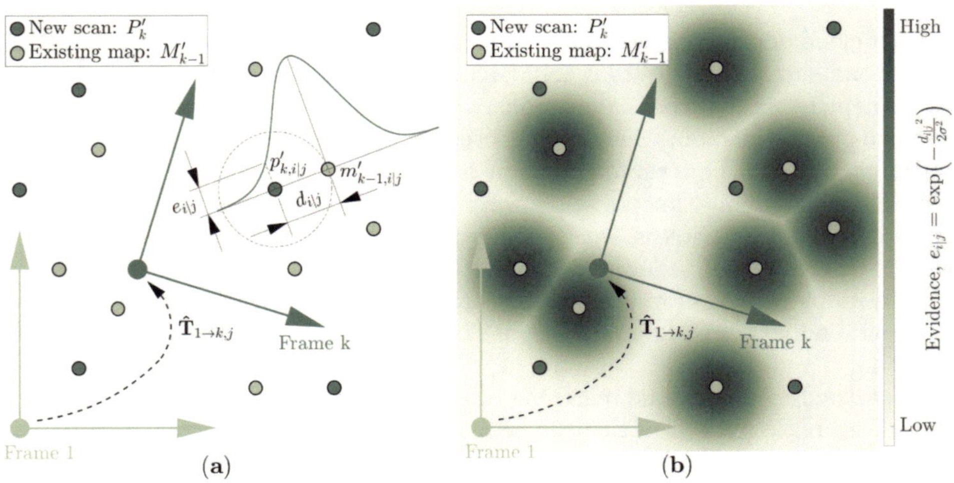

Figure 8.
(a) The k-th subsampled scan, $\mathbf{P}_{k'}$, is located by the j-th pose hypothesis, $\hat{\mathbf{T}}_{1\to k,j}$. The i-th point is depicted as $p'_{k,i|j}$ and the per-point evidence is calculated using its proximity, $d_{i|j}$, to the closest point, $m'_{k-1,i|j}$, in the existing map, $\mathbf{M}'_{k-1}$. Per-point evidence, $e_{i|j}$, is evaluated as a zero-mean Gaussian function of the distance between these points with a user-selected standard deviation, σ. (b) The selection of σ dictates the magnitude of evidence given the distance, $d_{i|j}$, between the scan and map points. Figure from Ref. [34].

algorithm requires a small configuration set. SiMpLE performs three steps to achieve accurate and timely odometry.

1. Input Scan Subsampling: The first step is to subsample the new scan at time k with a user-defined radius, r_{new}, to reduce the size of the input point cloud and allow for real-time computation (**Figure 8**).

2. Point cloud-to-map matching: A pose hypothesis, $\hat{\mathbf{T}}_{1\to k,j}$, is applied to the subsampled point cloud, P'_k, to locate it within the existing map, M'_{k-1}. Under this hypothesis, the approximate per-point evidence, $e_{i|j}$, for the i-th point, $p'_{k,i|j}$, is calculated by,

$$e_{i|j} = \exp\left(-\frac{d_{i|j}^2}{2\sigma^2}\right), \tag{9}$$

   where $d_{i|j}$ is the distance to the closest map point, $m'_{k,i|j}$. The evidence function has a user-selected standard deviation of σ. A search algorithm is used to find the hypothesis that maximizes the summated of these evidentials.

3. Local map update: The local map is updated with the current point cloud and the registration result from the previous step. The map is again subsampled at a user-defined radius of r_{map} to allow for fast matching in the next step and points outside the sensor's maximum range at the current pose are truncated to manage the map size.

6.4 Example odometry and mapping result

SiMpLE has been extensively tested on public benchmark datasets and performs among state-of-the-art algorithms with with least complex approach and smallest configuration set. An example result of real-time point cloud odometry is shown in **Figure 9**, using sequence 07 from the KITTI dataset [21]. The trajectory has 0.47% translation error, calculated using the method described in [21]. The vehicle's trajectory is displayed in white, and the corresponding stitched point cloud map is coloured by the point elevation.

SiMpLE's performance can be increased by fusing information from other sensing modalities (e.g. IMU) for providing information in between successive scans. The map currently generated simply stitches successive scans using the pose estimates, disregarding the presence of dynamic elements. SiMpLE can be augmented with dynamic object detection approaches to construct maps of the static environment, as demonstrated in [41]. The open-source approach is available from github.com/vb44/SiMpLE.

7. Application for sensor registration – SeREA

7.1 Problem relevance and description

A frequently occurring requirement for perception is the capacity to represent point cloud measurements in a different coordinate system. This requires accurate knowledge of the frame transform, $\hat{\mathbf{T}}_{\mathcal{P}\to\mathcal{S},j}$, between the desired coordinate system, $\mathcal{P}$, and the sensor coordinate system, $\mathcal{S}$, where the point cloud measurements, $\mathbf{P}_{\mathcal{S}}$, are directly provided (**Figure 1c**). For example, a mobile platform may need to interpret a point cloud to extract obstacles in a platform-fixed coordinate system where the geometry of the platform is described. Alternatively, point cloud measurements can be mapped to a navigation solution (e.g. RTK-GNSS) of the platform frame if the transform between platform and sensor, $\mathbf{T}_{\mathcal{P}\to\mathcal{S}}$, is known. The recovery of this transform is often called extrinsic calibration or sensor registration.

The sensor registration problem is commonly addressed using two strategies: (1) methods using a model of the environment and finding the sensor pose that best matches the sensor measurements captured at different positions to the model [20, 42], and (2) model-free approaches that aim to find the sensor pose that best aligns point clouds captured at different sensor poses [19, 43]. D'Adamo et al. [20] evaluate these approaches and find that model-based approaches provide greater accuracy but model-free approaches provide greater convenience by not requiring a model of the environment.

7.2 SeREA formulation

The previous section demonstrated that point clouds could be incrementally added to an existing map using an evidential approach. Hypothesized transforms between the map and scan, $\mathbf{T}_{\mathcal{P}\to\mathcal{S}}$, were evidenced if they located new points within proximity to existing map points. The Sensor Registration via Evidential Approximation (SeREA) approach, described here, is established on the same basis. The evidential registration problem is predicated on the belief that the most likely sensor registration, $\mathbf{T}^{\star}_{\mathcal{M}\to\mathcal{S}}$, is that which locates points from all scans within proximity to points of all other scans.

The algorithm does not require a survey or model of the environment. It seeks only to provide consistency between successive scans taken at m known platform locations, $\mathbf{T}_{\mathcal{W}\to\mathcal{P}_{1:m}}$, within a World coordinate system, $\mathcal{W}$.

Figure 9.
An example trajectory displayed in white and corresponding point cloud map from the KITTI dataset generated using SiMpLE. The trajectory exhibits low drift over a sequence of 1101 scans. The point cloud map is coloured by elevation.

The process is as follows:

1. Assuming the j-th registration hypothesis, $\hat{\mathbf{T}}_{\mathcal{P}\to\mathcal{S},j}$, locate all scans, $\mathbf{P}_{\mathcal{S},1:m}$, within the World coordinate frame, $\mathcal{W}$, using the known platform locations at each scan, $\mathbf{T}_{\mathcal{W}\to\mathcal{P}_{1:m}}$,

$$\mathbf{P}_{\mathcal{W},1:m} = \mathbf{T}_{\mathcal{W}\to\mathcal{P}_{1:m}} \hat{\mathbf{T}}_{\mathcal{P}\to\mathcal{S},j} \mathbf{P}_{\mathcal{S},1:m}. \tag{10}$$

2. Compute the evidence for each point in $\mathbf{P}_{\mathcal{W},1:m}$. The per-point evidence, $p_{\mathcal{W},i}$, under hypothesis, $\hat{\mathbf{T}}_{\mathcal{P}\to\mathcal{S},j}$, is given by,

$$e_{i|j} = \exp\left(-\frac{d_{i|j}^2}{2\sigma^2}\right), \tag{11}$$

where $d_{i|j}$ is the distance between point $p_{\mathcal{W},i}$ and its nearest neighbour in $\mathbf{P}_{\mathcal{W},1:m}$.

3. The total evidence for the j-th hypothesis is given by summating the evidence for each point.

4. The hypothesis space is searched for the pose corresponding to the maximum total evidence.

A pose search algorithm such as a particle filter or gradient-based solver is typically used in the final step when searching for the highest-scoring hypothesis. It is important to note that extracting the 6-DOF extrinsic parameters requires excitation of all degrees of freedom.

7.3 Example extrinsic calibration of a LiDAR mounted to a 6-DOF robot arm

An example is demonstrated below for registering a Velodyne VLP-16 LiDAR to a KUKA KR1000 Titan robotic manipulator. It is critical to accurately register the sensor as beliefs generated using the point cloud need to be transformed into the robot's frame to allow for interaction with the environment. For example, the robot may be required to identify a known geometry in the environment and then transport it between two locations. If the sensor's location relative to the robot is incorrect, the estimated object pose will also be incorrectly transformed from the sensor's frame to the robot's frame, resulting in failure.

Figure 10a illustrates the problem. The goal is to use a sequence of scans, $\mathbf{P}_{\mathcal{S}_{1:m}}$, captured in the Sensor frame, $\mathcal{S}$, along with the corresponding pose of the end-effector, $\mathbf{T}_{\mathcal{W}\to\mathcal{P}_{1:m}}$, in the World frame, $\mathcal{W}$, to estimate the sensor registration, $\hat{\mathbf{T}}_{\mathcal{P}\to\mathcal{S}}$. **Figure 9b** displays the end-effector's path over a sequence designed to excite all six degrees of freedom. The platform to sensor 6-DOF registration estimated using SeREA, and the comparison to machine drawings is listed in **Table 2**.

The machine drawings provide a reference to verify the accuracy of the registration result. In many typical applications, accurate drawings may not be available for comparison. In these circumstances, sensor registration estimation methods such as SeREA are required. **Figure 11** shows the resulting map produced with the sensor registration solution applied.

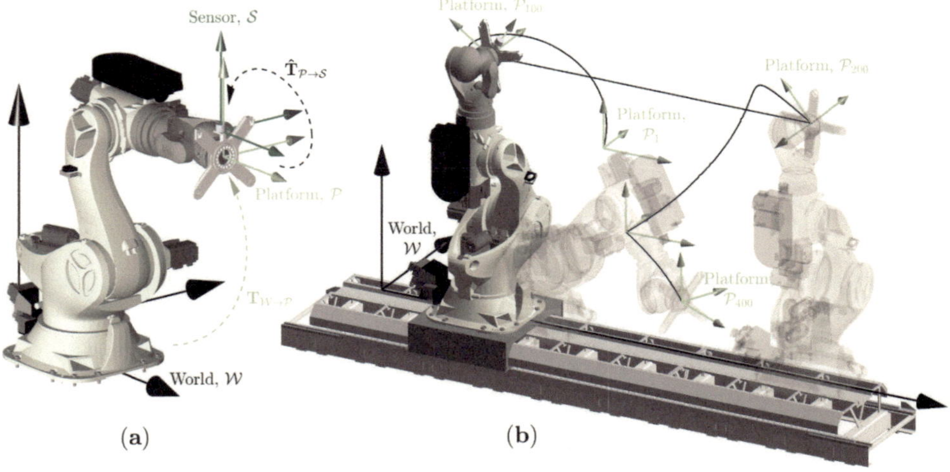

Figure 10.
A candidate sensor registration problem. (a) We seek to determine the frame transform, $\hat{\mathbf{T}}_{\mathcal{P}\to\mathcal{S}}$, that locates the installation of a LiDAR scanner (Sensor frame, $\mathcal{S}$) relative to an end-effector (Platform frame, $\mathcal{P}$). (b) The trajectory of the platform frame is excited in all 6-DOF. A kinematic solution is used to locate it relative to the World frame, $\mathcal{W}$.

Source	roll [deg]	pitch [deg]	yaw [deg]	x [mm]	y [mm]	z [mm]
Machine drawings	0.000	0.000	0.000	−40.000	0.000	250.000
SeREA estimate	0.000	0.082	0.049	−49.815	−4.672	258.851

Table 2.
A comparison of the sensor registration estimate and the machine drawings from which the LiDAR bracket was manufactured.

Figure 11.
The registration solution is applied, producing the point cloud shown. The SeREA approach seeks to provide consistency between successive scans.

8. Conclusions

A longstanding approach to interpreting point clouds is to use cost-based solutions. This chapter exposes the limitations of employing cost-based strategies, and promotes an alternative mode of extracting beliefs based in maximizing evidence. This leads to beliefs that are most likely to provide observed point cloud measurements. The change circumvents the need to perform additional processing (e.g. point cloud segmentation), and consequently reduces the complexity of the algorithm.

We formally define evidence as the likelihood of obtaining the observed point cloud measurements. However, this is challenging to use in real-time applications due to the computationally expensive raycasting operation. We demonstrate ways to rapidly approximate evidence and utilize this to provide real-time solutions to three commonly encountered perception problems: (i) PLuM for Pose estimation; (ii) SiMpLE for Scan matching; and (iii) SeREA for Sensor registration. All of which are based in a similar ideology.

The PLuM approach is demonstrated to locate known geometries in unsegmented data. A computational benefit is obtained by shifting from ray-based evidence to Cartesian-based evidence which can be readily looked up in pre-calculated tables. A limitation of this approximation is that it rewards points that are not feasibly obtained along the sensor's rays, e.g. a point on the opposite side of a model relative to the sensor is not feasible even though it is close to the model. Furthermore, PLuM does not provide diagnostics such as verifying the presence of the model and identifying if the model is different to what is expected.

The SiMpLE approach is shown to accurately map scans together with very low drift. However, the algorithm is unable to identify scenarios when the pose is degraded and due to the recursive nature, a single pose error is sufficient to offset the entire pose trajectory. Back-end methods can be used to correct the trajectory via loop closure.

The SeREA algorithm estimates extrinsic calibration parameters by maximizing the coherence between successive scans. A limitation of this approach is that the sensor needs to be excited in all six degrees of freedom.

The evidential approaches explored in this chapter present a pivotal change in the way beliefs are extracted from point cloud data. The solutions are found to be more robust to existing challenges and require much less configuration than cost-based approaches.

Author details

Vedant Bhandari*†, Tyson Phillips† and Ross McAree
School of Mechanical and Mining Engineering, The University of Queensland, Brisbane, Australia

*Address all correspondence to: v.bhandari@uq.edu.au

† These authors contributed equally.

References

[1] Besl P, McKay ND. A method for registration of 3-d shapes. IEEE Transactions on Pattern Analysis and Machine Intelligence. 1992;**14**(2):239-256

[2] Chen Y, Medioni G. Object modelling by registration of multiple range images. Image and Vision Computing. 1992; **10**(3):145-155. Range Image Understanding

[3] Biber P, Strasser W. The normal distributions transform: A new approach to laser scan matching. In: Proceedings 2003 IEEE/RSJ International Conference on Intelligent Robots and Systems (IROS 2003) (Cat. No.03CH37453). Vol. 3. New York City, United States: IEEE; 2003. pp. 2743–2748. DOI: 10.1109/IROS.2003.1249285

[4] Doyle AC, Paget S. The Adventure of Silver Blaze. UK: Mary McLaughlin and M. Einisman for the Scotland Yard Bookstore; 1979

[5] Sun R, Zhang E, Mu D, Ji S, Zhang Z, Liu H, et al. Optimization of the 3d point cloud registration algorithm based on fpfh features. Applied Sciences. 2023;**13** (5). Available from: https://www.mdpi.com/about/announcements/784

[6] Yu Y, Da F, Guo Y. Sparse icp with resampling and denoising for 3d face verification. IEEE Transactions on Information Forensics and Security. 2019;**14**(7):1917-1927

[7] Zhang J, Yao Y, Deng B. Fast and robust iterative closest point. IEEE Transactions on Pattern Analysis and Machine Intelligence. 2022;**44**(7): 3450-3466

[8] Donoso F, Austin K, McAree P. How do icp variants perform when used for scan matching terrain point clouds? Robotics and Autonomous Systems. 2017;**87**:147-161

[9] Donoso F, Austin K, McAree P. Three new iterative closest point variant-methods that improve scan matching for surface mining terrain. Robotics and Autonomous Systems. 2017;**95**:117-128

[10] Pomerleau F, Colas F, Siegwart R. A review of point cloud registration algorithms for mobile robotics. Foundations and Trends in Robotics. 2015;**4**(1):1-104

[11] Rusinkiewicz S, Levoy M. Efficient variants of the icp algorithm. In: Proceedings of the 3rd International Conference on 3-D Digital Imaging and Modeling. New York City, United States: IEEE; 2001. pp. 145-152. DOI: 10.1109/IM.2001.924423

[12] Myronenko A, Song X. Point set registration: Coherent point drift. IEEE Transactions on Pattern Analysis and Machine Intelligence. 2010;**32**(12): 2262-2275

[13] Kaminade T, Takubo T, Mae Y, Arai T. The generation of environmental map based on a ndt grid mapping - proposal of convergence calculation corresponding to high resolution grid. In: 2008 IEEE International Conference on Robotics and Automation. New York City, United States; 2008. pp. 1874-1879. DOI: 10.1109/ROBOT.2008.4543480

[14] Magnusson M, Lilienthal A, Duckett T. Scan registration for autonomous mining vehicles using 3d-ndt. Journal of Field Robotics. 2007; **24**(10):803-827

[15] Ahmadli I, Bedada WB, Palli G. Deep learning and octree-gpu-based icp for efficient 6d model registration of large

objects. In: Palli G, Melchiorri C, Meattini R, editors. Human-Friendly Robotics 2021. New York City, United States: Springer International Publishing; 2022. pp. 29-43. DOI: 10.1007/978-3-030-96359-0_3. ISBN: 978-3-030-96359-0

[16] Wang Y, Solomon JM. Deep closest point: Learning representations for point cloud registration. In: Proceedings of the IEEE/CVF International Conference on Computer Vision. Los Alamitos, CA, USA: IEEE Computer Society; 2019. pp. 3523-3532. DOI: 10.1109/ICCV.2019.00362

[17] Nouiraa H, Deschaud JE, Goulettea F. Point cloud refinement with a target-free intrinsic calibration of a mobile multi-beam lidar system. The International Archives of the Photogrammetry, Remote Sensing and Spatial Information Sciences. 2016; **XLI-B3**:359-366

[18] Bergelt R, Khan O, Hardt W. Improving the intrinsic calibration of a velodyne lidar sensor. In: 2017 IEEE Sensors. New York City, United States: IEEE; 2017. pp. 1-3. DOI: 10.1109/ICSENS.2017.8234357

[19] Sheehan M, Harrison A, Newman P. Self-calibration for a 3d laser. The International Journal of Robotics Research. 2012;**31**(5):675-687

[20] D'Adamo TA, Phillips TG, McAree PR. Registration of three-dimensional scanning lidar sensors: An evaluation of model-based and model-free methods. Journal of Field Robotics. 2018;**35**(7):1182-1200

[21] Geiger A, Lenz P, Urtasun R. Are we ready for autonomous driving? The KITTI vision benchmark suite. In: Conference on Computer Vision and Pattern Recognition (CVPR). New York City, United States: IEEE; 2012

[22] Phillips TG, Guenther N, McAree PR. When the dust settles: The four behaviors of lidar in the presence of fine airborne particulates. Journal of Field Robotics. 2017;**34**(5):985-1009

[23] Ouster. Os1 Mid-Range High-Resolution Imaging Lidar. 2023. Available from: https://data.ouster.io/downloads/datasheets/datasheet-rev7-v3p0-os1.pdf

[24] Pan Y, Xiao P, He Y, Shao Z, Li Z. MULLS: Versatile LiDAR SLAM via multi-metric linear least square. In: 2021 IEEE International Conference on Robotics and Automation (ICRA). New York City, United States: IEEE; 2021. pp. 11633-11640. DOI: 10.1109/ICRA48506.2021.9561364

[25] Phillips T, D'Adamo T, McAree P. Maximum sum of evidence—An evidence-based solution to object pose estimation in point cloud data. Sensors. 2021;**21**(19). Available from: https://www.mdpi.com/about/announcements/784

[26] Bhandari V, Phillips TG, McAree PR. Real-time 6-dof pose estimation of known geometries in point cloud data. Sensors. 2023;**23**(6). Available from: https://www.mdpi.com/about/announcements/784

[27] Li Y, Gu P. Free-form surface inspection techniques state of the art review. Computer-Aided Design. 2004; **36**(13):1395-1417

[28] Bertolazzi P, Liuzzi G, Guerra C. A global optimization algorithm for protein surface alignment. In: 2009 IEEE International Conference on Bioinformatics and Biomedicine Workshop. New York City, United States: IEEE; 2009. pp. 93-100. DOI: 10.1109/BIBMW.2009.5332143

[29] Stewart C, Tsai C-L, Roysam B. The dual-bootstrap iterative closest point algorithm with application to retinal image registration. IEEE Transactions on Medical Imaging. 2003;**22**(11):1379-1394

[30] Bashirov R, Ianina A, Iskakov K, Kononenko Y, Strizhkova V, Lempitsky V, et al. Real-time rgbd-based extended body pose estimation. In: Proceedings of the IEEE/CVF Winter Conference on Applications of Computer Vision. Los Alamitos, CA, USA: IEEE Computer Society; 2021. pp. 2807-2816

[31] Cui Y, An Y, Sun W, Hu H, Song X. Memory-augmented point cloud registration network for bucket pose estimation of the intelligent mining excavator. IEEE Transactions on Instrumentation and Measurement. 2022;**71**:1-12

[32] Borthwick JR. Mining Haul Truck Pose Estimation and Load Profiling Using Stereo Vision. [PhD thesis]. Vancouver: The University of British Columbia; 2003

[33] Yuan W, Choi D, Bolkas D. Gnss-imu-assisted colored icp for uav-lidar point cloud registration of peach trees. Computers and Electronics in Agriculture. 2022;**197**:106966

[34] Bhandari V, Phillips TG, McAree PR. Minimal configuration point cloud odometry and mapping. The International Journal of Robotics Research. DOI: 10.1177/02783649241235325

[35] Zhang J, Singh S. LOAM: Lidar odometry and mapping in real-time. In: Fox D, Kavraki LE, Kurniawati H, editors. Robotics: Science and Systems. Vol. 2. Berkeley, CA: Robotics: Science and Systems; 2014. pp. 1-9

[36] Yin D, Zhang Q, Liu J, Liang X, Wang Y, Maanp J, et al. Cae-lo: Lidar odometry leveraging fully unsupervised convolutional auto-encoder for interest point detection and feature description. ArXiv preprint. 2020. DOI: 10.48550/arXiv.2001.01354

[37] Chen X, Milioto A, Palazzolo E, Giguere P, Behley J, Stachniss C. Suma++: Efficient lidar-based semantic slam. In: 2019 IEEE/RSJ International Conference on Intelligent Robots and Systems (IROS). New York City, United States: IEEE; 2019. pp. 4530-4537. DOI: 10.1109/IROS40897.2019.8967704

[38] Chen G, Wang B, Wang X, Deng H, Wang B, Zhang S. Psf-lo: Parameterized semantic features based lidar odometry. In: 2021 IEEE International Conference on Robotics and Automation (ICRA). New York City, United States: IEEE; 2021. pp. 5056-5062. DOI: 10.1109/ICRA48506.2021.9561554

[39] Dellenbach P, Deschaud J-E, Jacquet B, Goulette F. CT-ICP: Real-time elastic LiDAR odometry with loop closure. In: 2022 International Conference on Robotics and Automation (ICRA). New York City, United States: IEEE; 2022. pp. 5580-5586

[40] Behley J, Stachniss C. Efficient surfel-based slam using 3d laser range data in urban environments. In: Kress-Gazit H, Srinivasa S, Howard T, Atanasov N, editors. Robotics: Science and Systems. Vol. 2018. Berkeley, CA: Robotics: Science and Systems; 2018. p. 59

[41] Kim G, Kim A. Remove, then revert: Static point cloud map construction using multiresolution range images. In: 2020 IEEE/RSJ International Conference on Intelligent Robots and Systems (IROS). New York City, United States:

IEEE; 2020. pp. 10758-10765. DOI: 10.1109/IROS45743.2020.9340856

[42] Phillips TG, Green ME, McAree PR. An adaptive structure filter for sensor registration from unstructured terrain. Journal of Field Robotics. 2015;**32**(5): 748-774

[43] Levinson J, Thrun S. Unsupervised Calibration for Multi-Beam Lasers. Berlin, Heidelberg: Springer Berlin Heidelberg; 2014. pp. 179-193

Chapter 3

Unmanned Aerial Systems (UAS)-Derived 3D Models for Digital Twin Construction Applications

Jhonattan G. Martinez, Luis A. Alarcon and Søren Wandahl

Abstract

The advent of Construction 4.0 has marked a paradigm shift in industrial development, integrating advanced technologies such as cyber-physical systems (CPS), sensors, unmanned aerial systems (UAS), building information modeling (BIM), and robotics. Notably, UASs have emerged as invaluable tools seamlessly embedded in construction processes, facilitating the comprehensive monitoring and digitization of construction projects from the early design phase through construction to the post-construction phases. Equipped with various sensors, such as imaging sensors, light detection and rangers (LiDAR), and thermal sensors, UASs play an important role in data collection processes, especially for 3D point cloud generation. Presently, UASs are recognized as one of the most effective means of generating a Digital Twin (DT) of construction projects, surpassing traditional methods in terms of speed and accuracy. This chapter provides a comprehensive overview of the applications of UAS-derived 3D models in DT, outlining their advantages and barriers and offering recommendations to augment their quality and accuracy.

Keywords: unmanned aerial systems (UAS), digital twin, construction industry, point cloud, photogrammetry, LiDAR, 3D model

1. Introduction

The advent of the construction 4.0 concept has ushered in a new era in industrial development, characterized by the integration of various technologies such as cyber-physical systems (CPS), sensors, building information modeling (BIM), robotics, big data, cloud manufacturing, virtual and augmented reality [1]. Among the various components of cyber-physical systems (CPS), unmanned aerial systems (UASs) stand out as valuable tools that can be seamlessly integrated into construction processes [2]. UASs can monitor and digitize construction projects throughout their lifecycle, starting from the early design phase, continuing through construction, and extending to post-construction phases. Integrating UASs in construction processes enhances efficiency and effectiveness in project management and execution [3].

A UAS stands for unmanned aircraft system. It refers to a complex system that includes an unmanned aircraft (UA), a drone, and all the necessary components and infrastructure for its operation [4]. UAS are commonly used for various applications, including aerial surveillance, photography, agriculture, search and rescue, scientific research, and commercial applications. They play a crucial role in a wide range of industries due to their adaptability and ability to access areas that may be dangerous or difficult for human pilots. The acceptance of UASs in the construction industry arises from their operational adaptability and capability to collect visual information dynamically and promptly. UAS can carry various sensors, which are crucial in collecting data and information from the environment during its operations. The type of sensors used can vary depending on the specific application and the data requirements of the flight mission. For instance, imaging sensors, light detection and rangers (LiDAR), thermal sensors, multispectral and hyperspectral sensors, and radar systems are some of the most common sensors used for the data collection process in construction [5]. Some of the UAS-derived products include aerial imagery, orthomosaic maps, digital elevation models (DEM), point clouds or 3D models, thermal maps, and inspection reports [6].

Nowadays, UASs are considered one of the most effective ways to create a Digital Twin (DT) of a construction project. This is because they can collect various types of data (e.g., images, videos, and point clouds) faster and with higher accuracy than traditional methods. DT is an interactive, real-time digital representation of building or infrastructure assets, employing sensors and cyber-physical systems to understand the physical world better [7]. Applying methods based on the DT concept has shown success, particularly in industries like manufacturing, where they have been effectively utilized for production planning and control. According to Tao et al. [8], a DT possesses three main elements: the physical object, the virtual element, and the link connections. Point clouds are crucial for creating and maintaining a DT because they provide a detailed and accurate representation of the physical environment [9]. Point clouds offer a highly detailed and precise 3D model of physical objects and their surroundings. Each point in the cloud corresponds to a specific location in space, accurately capturing the shape and geometry of surfaces.

Accordingly, this chapter aims to provide an overview of the application of UAS-derived 3D models in DT. The chapter describes the advantages and barriers to UAS applications for 3D point cloud generation and offers recommendations to enhance their quality and accuracy.

2. UAS applications in construction

A UAS, commonly called a drone, unpiloted aerial vehicle, or remotely piloted aircraft (RPA), is a powered aerial vehicle without a human operator on board (see **Figure 1**). It relies on aerodynamic forces for lifts, can operate autonomously or be controlled remotely, and can carry either lethal or nonlethal payloads [10]. The UAS's flight can be managed by onboard computers or a ground-based pilot in another vehicle. A UAS encompasses the aircraft and emphasizes the significance of additional elements such as sensors, control systems, control links, and a ground station. One of the fundamental parts of UASs is sensors. They enable UAS to gather data and perform specific tasks.

Figure 1.
Type of UASs: (a) fixed wing and (b) multi rotor.

Some of the most common sensors used in construction are imaging, LiDAR, and thermal sensors (see **Figure 2**) [11].

UASs have been incorporated into various construction-related tasks, as Ham et al. [12] outlined. Within the construction sector, UASs have been utilized for diverse purposes, including mapping and surveying construction sites [13], monitoring the progress of construction projects [14], safety inspections [15], inspecting structures [13], and conducting post-disaster assessment [16]. The integration of UASs into the construction industry is driven by the operational adaptability of aerial platforms and their ability to access areas that are difficult to reach or pose potential risks [17]. This adaptability allows UASs to contribute substantially across a spectrum of activities, from routine tasks such as site mapping and progress monitoring to critical functions like structural inspection and post-disaster assessment within the construction field.

In the construction stage, UASs are helpful, particularly in building inspection and progress monitoring [18]. Building inspection involves assessing a building's structural integrity, and the deployment of UAS during this phase offers several benefits, including cost reduction, time efficiency, and risk mitigation compared to traditional inspection methods like elevating platforms and scaffolding. UAS with high-resolution cameras can digitally monitor buildings, accurately detecting cracks and damages at a millimeter range [19]. This technology provides access to hard-to-reach areas, addressing the drawbacks of conventional methods, such as logistics time, safety hazards, and expensive equipment acquisition. The effectiveness of UAS in building inspection has been validated through comparisons with traditional methods. Various examples illustrate the versatility of UAS applications in building inspection, such as visualizing and assessing the condition of structures like stone-made church towers, hangar wall and roof joints, wind turbine cores, and chimneys for damage

Figure 2.
UAS-based sensors: (a) multispectral, (b) LiDAR, (c) thermal, and (d) imagery.

identification. Despite environmental challenges, UAS technology allows for detailed assessments, encouraging its use in such settings.

Integrating UASs can significantly enhance progress monitoring, involving tracking construction project advancements. Conventional monitoring methods, such as on-foot inspections and terrestrial or satellite imagery collection, face limitations due to factors like the time required for manual surveillance and environmental influences on satellite image quality [20]. UASs offer improved flexibility, high-resolution imagery, and operational proximity, enabling monitoring of construction sites across various periods. UASs have also been effectively utilized in monitoring the construction progress of roads and bridges within extensive infrastructure projects [16]. Unger et al. [21] utilized UAS-generated orthophotos to monitor specific building-zoned areas over 5 months, accurately identifying changes. The authors highlighted UAS technology as an efficient alternative to traditional photogrammetry for monitoring cost- and time-effective progress.

3. Digital Twin in construction

DT is a digital emulation of a tangible asset, employing DT-enabling technologies like sensors, communication networks, and 3D models to acquire real-time information and facilitate two-way coordination [22]. This ensures that the digital model is a counterpart to the physical asset. A DT relies on the fundamental principles of the Internet of Things (IoT) for its functionality [23]. The implementation of a DT is contingent upon the requisite level of information necessary to sustain and consistently update the model. As shown in **Figure 3**, A DT can be characterized by three main elements: (1) physical reality, (2) virtual representation, and (3) interconnections that exchange information among the physical and virtual counterparts [24].

Researchers have used the term DT in the construction domain as an equivalent of BIM models made in design and construction [25]. Other researchers perceive a DT as a digital representation of construction assets such as buildings, bridges, or industrial facilities [26]. However, such definitions fall short in describing a DT since they only consider the physical representation of the assets rather than the process and resources involved. A more accurate perspective defines a DT as a digital representation of resources, processes, or systems in the built or natural environment. This concept has been applied to all the construction stages, including design and engineering, construction, operation and maintenance, and demolition and recovery [27]. It has been used primarily in the construction stage to assess the structural integrity

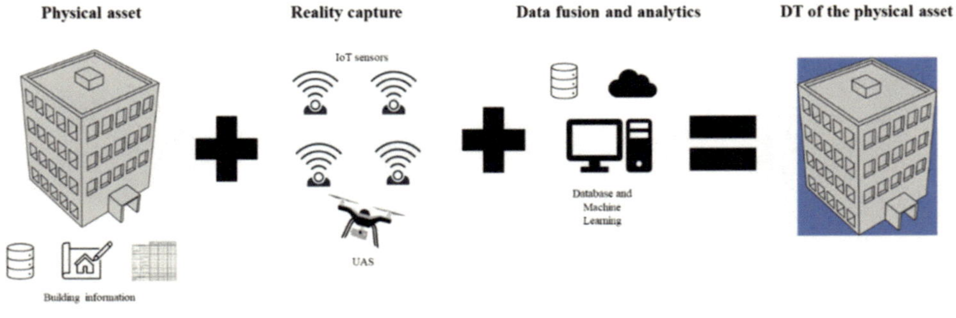

Figure 3.
DT representation.

of construction elements, control the actual and planned performance, and detect any deviation in the flows of materials, equipment, and labor [26]. Accordingly, DT could provide proactive and accurate status information on the construction site.

Various researchers have explored DT applications in construction. Barazzetti et al. [28] developed a historical building information model (HBIM) with augmented reality (AR) and virtual reality (VR) to boost cultural tourism. Gabor et al. [29] utilized DT for online planning and analyzed information flows within a cyber-physical system, enhancing engineering processes. Alonso et al. [30] focused on optimizing energy consumption in buildings' life cycles to reduce costs and environmental impact. Boje et al. [27] examined BIM applications in construction and outlined requirements for a new DT model. Lu et al. [31] developed a semi-automatic approach that determines an organized, accurate, and accessible DT system, combining images and computer aided design (CAD) drawings. Angjeliu et al. [32] instituted a technique to build an accurate digital model that reproduces experimental physical conditions. This model is used for exploring the structural response of the system, as well as for analyzing preventive maintenance and reinforcement procedures. The research addressed the methodological development of structural simulation, analysis, and control models for historic buildings by the DT concept. More recently, Pan and Zhang [33] devised and developed a data-driven DT framework integrating BIM, IoT, and data mining for advanced project management. The proposed framework aimed to enhance data communication and exploration to understand better, predict, and optimize physical construction processes.

4. UAS-derived 3D models for DT

Construction researchers and practitioners have shown increased interest in enhancing the accuracy of UAS-generated 3D models and, ideally, improving this technology's integration within construction practices [34]. High accuracy of 3D point clouds is required for various construction practices, including building surveying and digital construction site representation. 3D point clouds are crucial for creating and maintaining a DT because they provide a detailed and accurate representation of the physical environment. Some of the 3D-point cloud applications in DT are:

- *High-precision 3D representation:* Point clouds provide an intricately detailed and accurate three-dimensional portrayal of physical objects and their environment. Every individual point within the cloud corresponds to a precise spatial location, effectively capturing the surfaces' shape and geometry.

- *Reality capture:* Point clouds serve as a form of reality capture, allowing for the accurate documentation of the as-built environment. This is especially valuable in construction, architecture, and urban planning, where maintaining an up-to-date and accurate representation of the physical world is crucial.

- *Detailed spatial information:* Point clouds provide rich spatial information about the objects within their scope. This includes geometry and the relationships between elements, enabling a comprehensive understanding of physical space.

- *Integration with other data sources:* Point clouds can be integrated with data from other sensors and sources, such as images, LiDAR, or IoT devices. This integration enhances the DT's overall fidelity, providing a more comprehensive and holistic view of the physical environment.

- *Visualization and simulation:* The detailed information within point clouds facilitates realistic visualization and simulation within the DT. It allows users to investigate and analyze the environment virtually, helping in decision-making processes, planning, and simulations of various scenarios.

- *Monitoring changes over time:* A DT must reflect changes over time as a living representation of the physical world. Point clouds can be periodically updated to capture alterations in the physical environment, allowing for an accurate historical record and aiding in predictive analysis.

- *Asset management:* For infrastructure and facility management, point clouds provide essential data for maintaining and managing assets. They assist in assessing the condition of structures, planning maintenance, and optimizing operations.

Overall, 3D points clouds serve as a foundational element for a DT, offering the intricate spatial details necessary for creating a realistic and dynamic virtual replica of the physical world. This accuracy is vital for urban planning and construction applications to facility management.

5. Techniques to generate 3D point cloud data for DT

There are two main techniques to generate 3D point clouds of the construction site: photogrammetry and LiDAR-based mapping.

5.1 UAS-based photogrammetry

Photogrammetry is a technique used to extract geometric information from two-dimensional images or photographs. It encompasses analyzing the positions and relationships of points in multiple images to create a three-dimensional representation of the photographed object or scene [35]. This process relies on the principles of triangulation, where the positions of points are determined by measuring the angles formed by the lines of sight to those points from known positions.

UAS-based photogrammetry offers several advantages over traditional photogrammetry methods. UAS provides the flexibility to capture images from various angles and altitudes, allowing for more comprehensive coverage of an area. Besides, using UAS can significantly reduce costs compared with survey methods or ground-based surveying [36]. This is because they can cover more areas in less time and faster than other survey methods. Another advantage of using UASs is their ability to capture high-resolution images, leading to detailed and accurate mapping results. This is especially beneficial for applications requiring precise measurements or identifying small features [37]. UAS-based photogrammetry begins with the data collection process. It is important to define the area to be surveyed properly during this. Flight altitude, overlap settings, and camera parameters are essential for optimal image acquisition. Once the data is collected, the raw data is processed, considering parameters like camera calibration, camera alignment, and coordinate system. The data rectified is later reconstructed to generate a dense point cloud by triangulating the positions of identified features in multiple images (see **Figure 4**).

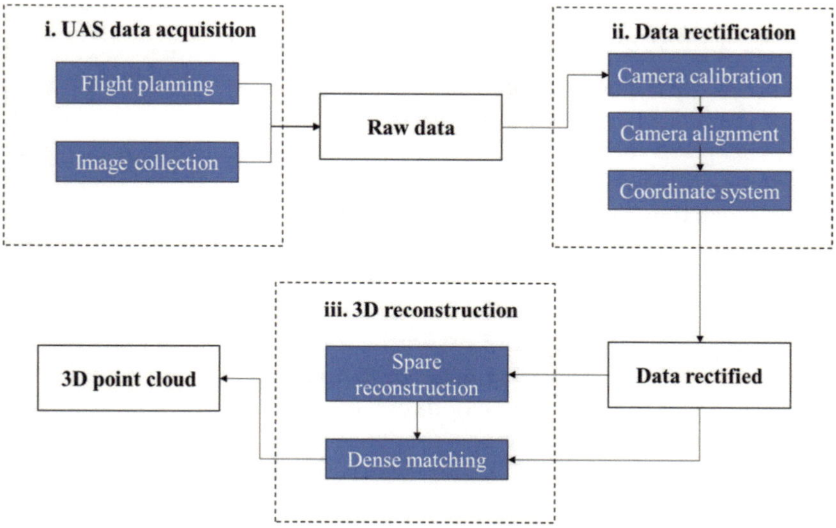

Figure 4.
UAS-based photogrammetry workflow.

5.2 UAS LiDAR-based mapping

Lidar-based mapping is a remote sensing technology that uses laser light to calculate distances and create detailed, three-dimensional maps of the Earth's surface [38]. LiDAR-based mapping involves deploying a LiDAR sensor to gather precise and accurate elevation data, enabling the creation of high-resolution topographic maps, digital terrain models (DTMs), and 3D representations of the environment [39]. LiDAR-based technology is characterized by its high precision and accuracy, rapid data collection, day and night operation capabilities, data density and resolution, and ability to create realistic representations of the environment. Like UAS-based photogrammetry, UAS LiDAR-based mapping requires planning the flight mission and considering the flight altitude, speed, and overlap setting. A pre-flight check is recommended to ensure the UAS, and the LiDAR sensors are well calibrated. During the data collection, LiDAR sensors will emit laser pulses toward the ground, and the system records the time it takes for the pulses to return, calculating distances. After that, the data is uploaded into software to filter, classify, and organize the point cloud. The final step consists of removing noise, classifying ground and non-ground points, and enhancing data quality.

6. Improving UAS photogrammetry-based 3D point clouds

Various methods and techniques can be used to enhance 3D point clouds for DT applications. Those methods involve optimizing multiple data acquisition, processing, and post-processing aspects. Here are several strategies to improve the accuracy of UAS-derived point clouds, including:

Use ground control points (GCP) to improve spatial accuracy: GCPs are spots of known position strategically located in a place of interest. Such points could achieve a 3D point cloud accuracy of up to 5 centimeters [40]. Nevertheless, this approach is characterized as a time-consuming and labor-intensive process. In classic photogrammetry, GCP must be distributed uninformedly throughout the whole area and the center. A study conducted by Sanz-Ablanedo et al. [41] demonstrated that 3D point cloud accuracy depends on the location and the number of GCPs used during reconstruction. GCPs are often used to increase the positioning accuracy of the UAS-derived 3D point clouds. Commercially available off-the-shelf UAS are commonly equipped with a single-frequency global navigation satellite system (GNSS) (L1) device, which limits positioning accuracy, typically ranging from 1 to 25 meters [42]. Nevertheless, specific construction applications, especially DT-related ones, demand higher precision. To address this, a common approach involves identifying critical features in the 3D point clouds that can be matched to known real-world coordinates using GCP [40]. **Figure 5** presents a scenario in which four GCPs were placed to enhance the 3D point cloud accuracy of the building. The experiment aimed to compare the accuracy of 3D point clouds created with and without using GCP.

Use real-time kinematic (RTK) or post-processing kinematic (PPK) to enhance the geometric accuracy: Unlike GCPs, RTK and PPK methods utilize single-frequency GNSS (L1) or dual-frequency GNSS (L1/L2) receivers, offering positioning accuracy ranging from 1 to 30 centimeters and eliminating the need for GCPs, thus saving time and costs significantly [40, 43]. RTK corrects positioning coordinates during flight, while PPK applies corrections post-flight [44]. Dual-frequency GNSS receivers are preferred over single-frequency ones due to their ability to address ionospheric and tropospheric effects, resulting in higher accuracy in UAS-generated 3D point clouds [45]. RTK technology provides instant access to rover position and solution quality information, facilitating informed decision-making during field operations. It also saves time on post-processing calculations compared to PPK. However, RTK requires a live radio link between the reference station and rover, adding equipment and setup costs and complexity to the UAS payload. Loss of this link poses a risk of losing differentially corrected rover positions. In contrast, PPK operations do not require live links, simplifying logistics and reducing risk.

Use of high-resolution RGB sensors: the UAS's camera resolution is crucial in determining the accuracy of 3D point reconstruction [46]. A better camera resolution reduces the ground sample distance (GSD) during the data collection. In remote sensing, GSD refers to the space on the ground that each pixel in the image represents [47]. Higher-resolution cameras have smaller pixels, resulting in a smaller GSD. Smaller GSD allows for the differentiation of finer details in the scene, leading to more accurate and precise reconstruction of 3D points. Besides, a high camera

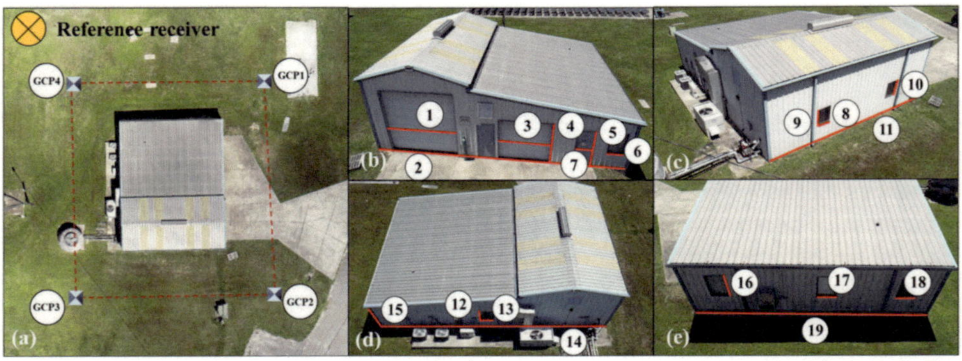

Figure 5.
Use of GCP to improve the 3D point cloud accuracy.

resolution allows for capturing more information and features in the images. This increased level of detail enables the photogrammetric software to identify and match more distinct points in the images, contributing to a more accurate reconstruction of the 3D scene.

On the other hand, higher-resolution images also provide more overlap and redundancy in the captured data, allowing for better triangulation and more accurate determination of 3D point positions. This aspect improves measurement precision, especially when determining distances between points in the images. This precision translates into more accurate 3D coordinates for the reconstructed points.

Proper flight mission design: a proper flight mission is essential to guarantee an adequate data collection process. Initially, it is critical to define the overlap percentage between images. A higher overlap between images (both along-track and across-track) ensures more redundant information for accurate feature matching and 3D reconstruction, helping to create a denser point cloud [48]. At the same time, it is vital to guarantee that the images adequately cover the entire area of interest. Gaps or missing sections can lead to incomplete or inaccurate point clouds. Another important aspect is the camera orientation and angle of view. For instance, nadir (straight-down) imagery suits top-down mapping, while oblique imagery can provide more details for vertical structures. The choice depends on the application, but combining both might enhance accuracy and completeness. Flight altitude determines the GSD, which in turn affects the accuracy of the 3D point cloud. Lower altitudes with smaller GSD can capture finer details but might require more flight lines for complete coverage. Finally, flight patterns, such as a grid or spiral, impact the distribution of images and the redundancy in coverage. A well-designed pattern ensures optimal overlap and helps overcome challenges like occlusions and shadows.

Proper camera calibration: the calibration process involves determining a camera's intrinsic and extrinsic parameters, which helps correct distortions and aligns the camera's view with the real-world coordinates [49]. Camera calibration enhances 3D point cloud accuracy and quality by correcting distortions, determining intrinsic and extrinsic parameters, aligning coordinates, and reducing systematic errors. It ensures that the 3D reconstruction accurately represents real-world dimensions and relationships, improving depth accuracy and providing reliable spatial information for various applications.

7. UAS LiDAR-based 3D point clouds enhancement

The generation process of 3D point clouds derived from LiDAR data collected by UAS involves several steps to improve data quality, accuracy, and interpretability. Here is a short explanation of the process of generation of LiDAR-based 3D point clouds:

- *Remove the noise:* LiDAR data often contains noise caused by various factors such as sensor inaccuracies, environmental conditions, or object interference [50]. Filtering techniques like statistical outlier removal or voxel-based filtering can help eliminate noise points from the point cloud.

- *Point cloud registration:* If the LiDAR data is collected from multiple flight passes or from different sensors, aligning and registering the point clouds into a single coordinate system is necessary [51]. Iterative closest point (ICP) algorithms or feature-based registration methods can be used for point cloud registration.

- *Data fusion:* Combining LiDAR data with other datasets like imagery or GIS data can provide additional context and improve the point cloud interpretation [52]. Techniques such as sensor fusion or data integration can be employed for this purpose.

- *Colorization:* Adding color information to the point cloud can enhance visualization and interpretation [53]. This can be achieved by integrating imagery data collected concurrently with LiDAR or by using image-based methods to colorize the point cloud.

- *Quality assessment and control:* Performing quality assessment and control measures to identify and correct errors or artifacts in the point cloud is essential [54]. This can involve visual inspection, comparing against ground truth data, or using automated validation algorithms.

8. Advantages and disadvantages of using UAS-based photogrammetry and UAS LiDAR-based mapping for DT

UAS-based photogrammetry and UAS LiDAR-based mapping are powerful tools for the real-time digitalization of construction job sites. Nevertheless, factors such as deployment cost, environmental conditions, payload capacity, and flight regulation can significantly influence the impact of such technologies for DT-related applications. On the one hand, UAS-based photogrammetry offers cost-effectiveness, flexibility, and accessibility, with the ability to access remote areas swiftly. It provides high-resolution imagery for detailed mapping and analysis, along with real-time data processing capabilities, facilitating immediate decision-making. Moreover, its rapid deployment capability allows for quick response to changing project needs or emergencies, ensuring near-instantaneous data acquisition. On the other hand, UAS LiDAR-based mapping enables efficient data collection over vast areas, reducing field time. Additionally, LiDAR generates accurate 3D point clouds, allowing for detailed analysis and visualization of terrain features. Its suitability for mapping complex terrain, including urban areas, forests, and rugged landscapes, makes it particularly advantageous where traditional photogrammetry may be limited.

Nevertheless, the application of UAS-based photogrammetry for DT is highly dependent on weather conditions. Unfavorable conditions can introduce errors, distortions, and limitations during data acquisition. To ensure precision, it is crucial to use sensors designed for robustness in diverse conditions, employ appropriate calibration and filtering techniques, and consider environmental factors during data collection [55]. Adequate lighting is essential for precise depth sensing, and issues such as low light or strong shadows can lead to inaccuracies in in-depth measurements and impact overall 3D point cloud quality. To address these challenges, controlled lighting setups or sensors designed for varied lighting conditions can be beneficial. Outdoor settings are particularly susceptible to weather conditions affecting data quality. For instance, rain, snow, or fog can scatter or absorb light, reducing sensor range and accuracy. Advanced sensors with features like adaptive filtering or environmental compensation can help mitigate the impact of adverse weather conditions. Moreover, temperature and humidity fluctuations can influence sensor performance, potentially causing thermal expansion or contraction that alters internal geometry. Maintaining a stable environmental temperature and humidity level is imperative for consistent and accurate 3D data acquisition. UAS platforms have limited payload capacity, restricting the types of sensors and equipment that can be carried. This can limit the versatility of UAS-based photogrammetry solutions.

UAS LiDAR-based mapping solutions present challenges including high cost due to expensive LiDAR sensors and complex and time-consuming data processing that requires specialized expertise. Besides, dealing with highly reflective surfaces, such as glass or water, poses challenges in in-depth sensing, as reflections can lead to inaccurate depth measurements and artifacts in the 3D point cloud. Specialized algorithms or sensors with enhanced capabilities for handling reflective surfaces are essential for achieving precise 3D reconstructions.

For both approaches, UAS flight regulations can significantly impact the quality and accuracy of point clouds generated through photogrammetry or LiDAR. Compliance with regulations is essential to ensure safe and legal UAS operations, and these regulations can influence the data collection process and subsequent data quality [56]. Regulatory restrictions on maximum flight altitudes may affect the resolution of the captured imagery or LiDAR data. Higher altitudes can result in lower point cloud density, potentially reducing the level of detail in the reconstruction. Besides, regulations may impose constraints on flight patterns and the area that can be covered during a single flight. Compliance with these boundaries may impact the completeness and accuracy of the point cloud, particularly for large or complex survey areas. UAS regulations often define no-fly zones around airports or critical infrastructure. These restrictions can limit data collection in certain areas, affecting the overall coverage and accuracy of the point cloud.

Another important aspect of the UAS flight is the operational hours. Guidelines may specify permissible operational hours for UAS flights. Adhering to these timeframes is crucial, as variations in lighting conditions (e.g., sunrise and sunset) can influence image quality and, consequently, point cloud accuracy. Moreover, compliance with safety regulations, including collision avoidance measures, can impact flight paths and speed. Safe flight practices are essential to prevent accidents that could lead to data loss or inaccuracies in the point cloud. Finally, collaborating with relevant authorities and obtaining necessary permits is essential for planning UAS surveys. Understanding and adhering to regulatory requirements during the planning phase is critical for accurate and legally compliant data collection.

9. Conclusions

This chapter provides an overview of the application of UAS-derived 3D models in DT by describing the advantages and barriers of its applications for generating 3D point clouds. Moreover, the chapter provides insights to enhance the UAS-based 3D point clouds for DT applications. Using UASs in construction as a data collection system provides enormous benefits by reducing the cost and time to generate 3D point clouds. The data gathered by UAS provides a high-precision 3D representation and rich spatial information on the physical asset. These aspects classify UAS as fundamental tools for applications related to DT in construction. Two techniques to generate 3D point clouds stand out over traditional mapping techniques. On the one hand, UAS-based photogrammetry is accessible and cost-effective, allows rapid data collection, and provides real-time construction site monitoring. On the other hand, UAS LiDAR-based mapping offers high-precision 3D mapping and efficient data processing and reduces GCP requirements.

Despite the many advantages of both approaches, challenges persist in addressing safety concerns, privacy issues, and regulatory compliance when deploying UASs within the construction industry. This is particularly crucial given the likelihood of a significant population residing and working in the deployment areas. To address these challenges effectively, it is advised to incorporate frequent routine training sessions and conduct thorough risk assessments as integral components of any UAS deployment. This proactive approach aims to minimize the impact of using UASs in the construction domain.

Author details

Jhonattan G. Martinez[1*], Luis A. Alarcon[2] and Søren Wandahl[1]

1 Aarhus University, Aarhus, Denmark

2 Pontifical University Catholic of Chile, Santiago, Chile

*Address all correspondence to: jgmartinez@cae.au.dk

References

[1] Forcael E, Ferrari I, Opazo-Vega A, Pulido-Arcas JA. Construction 4.0: A literature review. Sustainability. 2020;**12**:9755. DOI: 10.3390/su12229755

[2] Gheisari M, Costa DB, Irizarry J. Unmanned aerial system applications in construction. In: Construction 4.0. United Kingdom: Routledge; 2020

[3] Rakha T, Gorodetsky A. Review of Unmanned Aerial System (UAS) applications in the built environment: Towards automated building inspection procedures using drones. Automation in Construction. 2018;**93**:252-264. DOI: 10.1016/j.autcon.2018.05.002

[4] Albeaino G, Gheisari M. Trends, benefits, and barriers of unmanned aerial systems in the construction industry: A survey study in the United States. Journal of Information Technology in Construction. 2021;**26**:84-111. DOI: 10.36680/j.itcon.2021.006

[5] Toth C, Jóźków G. Remote sensing platforms and sensors: A survey. ISPRS Journal of Photogrammetry and Remote Sensing. 2016;**115**:22-36. DOI: 10.1016/j.isprsjprs.2015.10.004

[6] Pricope NG, Mapes KL, Woodward KD, Olsen SF, Baxley JB. Multi-sensor assessment of the effects of varying processing parameters on UAS product accuracy and quality. Drones. 2019;**3**:63. DOI: 10.3390/drones3030063

[7] Lopez V, Akundi A. A conceptual model-based systems engineering (MBSE) approach to develop digital twins. In: 2022 IEEE International Systems Conference (SysCon), Montreal, QC, Canada. 2022. pp. 1-5. DOI: 10.1109/SysCon53536.2022.9773869

[8] Tao F, Sui F, Liu A, Qi Q, Zhang M, Song B, et al. Digital twin-driven product design framework. International Journal of Production Research. 2019;**57**:3935-3953. DOI: 10.1080/00207543.2018.1443229

[9] Xue F, Lu W, Chen Z, Webster CJ. From LiDAR point cloud towards digital twin city: Clustering city objects based on Gestalt principles. ISPRS Journal of Photogrammetry and Remote Sensing. 2020;**167**:418-431. DOI: 10.1016/j.isprsjprs.2020.07.020

[10] Vergouw B, Nagel H, Bondt G, Custers B. Drone technology: Types, payloads, applications, frequency spectrum issues and future developments. In: Custers B, editor. The Future of Drone Use: Opportunities and Threats from Ethical and Legal Perspectives. The Hague: T.M.C. Asser Press; 2016. pp. 21-45. DOI: 10.1007/978-94-6265-132-6_2

[11] Rao AS, Radanovic M, Liu Y, Hu S, Fang Y, Khoshelham K, et al. Real-time monitoring of construction sites: Sensors, methods, and applications. Automation in Construction. 2022;**136**:104099. DOI: 10.1016/j.autcon.2021.104099

[12] Ham Y, Han KK, Lin JJ, Golparvar-Fard M. Visual monitoring of civil infrastructure systems via camera-equipped Unmanned Aerial Vehicles (UAVs): A review of related works. Visualization in Engineering. 2016;**4**:1. DOI: 10.1186/s40327-015-0029-z

[13] Álvares JS, Costa DB, de Melo RRS. Exploratory study of using unmanned aerial system imagery for construction site 3D mapping. Construction Innovation. 2018;**18**:301-320. DOI: 10.1108/CI-05-2017-0049

[14] Jacob-Loyola N, Muñoz-La Rivera F, Herrera RF, Atencio E. Unmanned aerial vehicles (UAVs) for physical progress monitoring of construction. Sensors. 2021;**21**:4227. DOI: 10.3390/s21124227

[15] Martinez JG, Gheisari M, Alarcón LF. UAV integration in current construction safety planning and monitoring processes: Case study of a high-rise building construction project in Chile. Journal of Management in Engineering. 2020;**36**:05020005. DOI: 10.1061/(ASCE) ME.1943-5479.0000761

[16] Ezequiel CAF, Cua M, Libatique NC, Tangonan GL, Alampay R, Labuguen RT, et al. UAV aerial imaging applications for post-disaster assessment, environmental management and infrastructure development. In: 2014 International Conference on Unmanned Aircraft Systems (ICUAS), Orlando, FL, USA: IEEE; May 2014. pp. 274-283. DOI: 10.1109/ICUAS.2014.6842266

[17] Albeaino G, Gheisari M, Franz B. A systematic review of unmanned aerial vehicle application areas and technologies in the AEC domain. The Electronic Journal of Information Technology in Construction. 2019;**24**:381-405

[18] Lin JJ, Han KK, Golparvar-Fard M. A framework for model-driven acquisition and analytics of visual data using UAVs for automated construction progress monitoring. In: Computing in Civil Engineering. 2015. pp. 156-164. n.d. DOI: 10.1061/9780784479247.020

[19] Mader D, Blaskow R, Westfeld P, Weller C. Potential of UAV-based laser scanner and multispectral camera data in building inspection. The International Archives of the Photogrammetry, Remote Sensing and Spatial Information Sciences. 2016;**XLI-B1**:1135-1142. DOI: 10.5194/ isprs-archives-XLI-B1-1135-2016

[20] Zhou Z, Irizarry J, Lu Y. A multidimensional framework for unmanned aerial system applications in construction project management. Journal of Management in Engineering. 2018;**34**:04018004. DOI: 10.1061/(ASCE) ME.1943-5479.0000597

[21] Unger J, Reich M, Heipke C. UAV-based photogrammetry: Monitoring of a building zone. The International Archives of the Photogrammetry, Remote Sensing and Spatial Information Sciences. 2014;**XL-5**(5):601-606. DOI: 10.15488/892

[22] Madubuike OC, Anumba CJ, Khallaf R. A review of digital twin applications in construction. Journal of Information Technology in Construction. 2022;**27**:145-172. DOI: 10.36680/j. itcon.2022.008

[23] Datta SPA. Emergence of Digital Twins—Is this the march of reason? Journal of Innovation Management. 2017;**5**:14-33. DOI: 10.24840/2183-0606_005.003_0003

[24] VanDerHorn E, Mahadevan S. Digital twin: Generalization, characterization and implementation. Decision Support Systems. 2021;**145**:113524. DOI: 10.1016/j. dss.2021.113524

[25] Aengenvoort K, Krämer M. BIM in the operation of buildings. In: Borrmann A, König M, Koch C, Beetz J, editors. Building Information Modeling: Technology Foundations and Industry Practice. Cham: Springer International Publishing; 2018. pp. 477-491. DOI: 10.1007/978-3-319-92862-3_29

[26] Opoku D-GJ, Perera S, Osei-Kyei R, Rashidi M. Digital twin application in the construction industry: A literature review. Journal of Building Engineering. 2021;**40**:102726. DOI: 10.1016/j. jobe.2021.102726

[27] Boje C, Guerriero A, Kubicki S, Rezgui Y. Towards a semantic Construction Digital Twin: Directions for future research. Automation in Construction. 2020;**114**:103179. DOI: 10.1016/j.autcon.2020.103179

[28] Barazzetti L, Banfi F, Brumana R, Oreni D, Previtali M, Roncoroni F. HBIM and augmented information: Towards a wider user community of image and range-based reconstructions. The International Archives of the Photogrammetry, Remote Sensing and Spatial Information Sciences. 2015;**40**:35-42

[29] Gabor T, Belzner L, Kiermeier M, Beck MT, Neitz A. A simulation-based architecture for smart cyber-physical systems. In: 2016 IEEE International Conference on Autonomic Computing (ICAC). 2016. pp. 374-379. DOI: 10.1109/ICAC.2016.29

[30] Alonso R, Borras M, Koppelaar RHEM, Lodigiani A, Loscos E, Yöntem E. SPHERE: BIM digital twin platform. Proceedings. 2019;**20**:9. DOI: 10.3390/proceedings2019020009

[31] Lu Q, Chen L, Li S, Pitt M. Semi-automatic geometric digital twinning for existing buildings based on images and CAD drawings. Automation in Construction. 2020;**115**:103183. DOI: 10.1016/j.autcon.2020.103183

[32] Angjeliu G, Coronelli D, Cardani G. Development of the simulation model for Digital Twin applications in historical masonry buildings: The integration between numerical and experimental reality. Computers & Structures. 2020;**238**:106282. DOI: 10.1016/j.compstruc.2020.106282

[33] Pan Y, Zhang L. A BIM-data mining integrated digital twin framework for advanced project management. Automation in Construction. 2021;**124**:103564. DOI: 10.1016/j.autcon.2021.103564

[34] Malihi S, Valadan Zoej MJ, Hahn M. Large-scale accurate reconstruction of buildings employing point clouds generated from UAV imagery. Remote Sensing. 2018;**10**:1148. DOI: 10.3390/rs10071148

[35] Gini R, Pagliari D, Passoni D, Pinto L, Sona G, Dosso P. UAV photogrammetry: Block triangulation comparisons. The International Archives of the Photogrammetry, Remote Sensing and Spatial Information Sciences. 2013;**XL-1-W2**:157-162. DOI: 10.5194/isprsarchives-XL-1-W2-157-2013

[36] Kršák B, Blišťan P, Pauliková A, Puškárová P, Kovanič Ľ, Palková J, et al. Use of low-cost UAV photogrammetry to analyze the accuracy of a digital elevation model in a case study. Measurement. 2016;**91**:276-287. DOI: 10.1016/j.measurement.2016.05.028

[37] Saadatseresht M, Hashempour AH, Hasanlou M. UAV photogrammetry: A practical solution for challenging mapping projects. The International Archives of the Photogrammetry, Remote Sensing and Spatial Information Sciences. 2015;**XL-1-W5**:619-623. DOI: 10.5194/isprsarchives-XL-1-W5-619-2015

[38] Pricope NG, Halls JN, Mapes KL, Baxley JB, Wu JJ. Quantitative comparison of UAS-Borne LiDAR systems for high-resolution forested wetland mapping. Sensors. 2020;**20**:4453. DOI: 10.3390/s20164453

[39] Li X, Liu C, Wang Z, Xie X, Li D, Xu L. Airborne LiDAR: State-of-the-art of system design, technology and application. Measurement Science and Technology. 2020;**32**:032002. DOI: 10.1088/1361-6501/abc867

[40] Bolkas D. Assessment of GCP number and separation distance for small UAS surveys with and without GNSS-PPK positioning. Journal of Surveying Engineering. 2019;**145**:04019007. DOI: 10.1061/(ASCE)SU.1943-5428.0000283

[41] Sanz-Ablanedo E, Chandler JH, Rodríguez-Pérez JR, Ordóñez C. Accuracy of Unmanned Aerial Vehicle (UAV) and SfM photogrammetry survey as a function of the number and location of ground control points used. Remote Sensing. 2018;**10**:1606. DOI: 10.3390/rs10101606

[42] Yao H, Clark RL. Evaluation of sub-meter and 2 to 5 meter accuracy GPS receivers to develop digital elevation models. Precision Agriculture. 2000;**2**:189-200. DOI: 10.1023/A:1011429815226

[43] Fazeli H, Samadzadegan F, Dadrasjavan F. Evaluating the potential of RTK-UAV for automatic point cloud generation in 3D rapid mapping. The International Archives of the Photogrammetry, Remote Sensing and Spatial Information Sciences. 2016;**XLI-B6**:221-226. DOI: 10.5194/isprs-archives-XLI-B6-221-2016

[44] Tomaštík J, Mokroš M, Surový P, Grznárová A, Merganič J. UAV RTK/PPK method—An optimal solution for mapping inaccessible forested areas? Remote Sensing. 2019;**11**:721. DOI: 10.3390/rs11060721

[45] Deng Z, Bender M, Zus F, Ge M, Dick G, Ramatschi M, et al. Validation of tropospheric slant path delays derived from single and dual frequency GPS receivers. Radio Science. 2011;**46**:1-11. DOI: 10.1029/2011RS004687

[46] da Silva Neto JG, da Lima Silva PJ, Figueredo F, Teixeira JMXN, Teichrieb V. Comparison of RGB-D sensors for 3D reconstruction. In: 2020 22nd Symposium on Virtual and Augmented Reality (SVR), Porto de Galinhas, Brazil. 2020. pp. 252-261. DOI: 10.1109/SVR51698.2020.00046

[47] Tahar KN. An evaluation on different number of ground control points in unmanned aerial vehicle photogrammetric block. The International Archives of the Photogrammetry, Remote Sensing and Spatial Information Sciences. 2013;**XL-2-W2**:93-98. DOI: 10.5194/isprsarchives-XL-2-W2-93-2013

[48] Biundini IZ, Pinto MF, Melo AG, Marcato ALM, Honório LM, Aguiar MJR. A framework for coverage path planning optimization based on point cloud for structural inspection. Sensors. 2021;**21**:570. DOI: 10.3390/s21020570

[49] Cramer M, Przybilla H-J, Zurhorst A. UAV cameras: Overview and geometric calibration benchmark. The International Archives of the Photogrammetry, Remote Sensing and Spatial Information Sciences. 2017;**XLII-2-W6**:85-92. DOI: 10.5194/isprs-archives-XLII-2-W6-85-2017

[50] Zeybek M, Şanlıoğlu İ. Point cloud filtering on UAV based point cloud. Measurement. 2019;**133**:99-111. DOI: 10.1016/j.measurement.2018.10.013

[51] Shao J, Yao W, Wan P, Luo L, Wang P, Yang L, et al. Efficient co-registration of UAV and ground LiDAR forest point clouds based on canopy shapes. International Journal of Applied Earth Observation and Geoinformation. 2022;**114**:103067. DOI: 10.1016/j.jag.2022.103067

[52] Elamin A, El-Rabbany A. UAV-based multi-sensor data fusion for urban land cover mapping using a deep

convolutional neural network. Remote Sensing. 2022;**14**:4298. DOI: 10.3390/rs14174298

[53] Xu J, Yao C, Ma H, Qian C, Wang J. Automatic point cloud colorization of ground-based LiDAR data using video imagery without position and orientation system. Remote Sensing. 2023;**15**:2658. DOI: 10.3390/rs15102658

[54] Pereira LG, Fernandez P, Mourato S, Matos J, Mayer C, Marques F. Quality control of outsourced LiDAR data acquired with a UAV: A case study. Remote Sensing. 2021;**13**:419. DOI: 10.3390/rs13030419

[55] Long N, Millescamps B, Pouget F, Dumon A, Lachaussée N, Bertin X. Accuracy assessment of coastal topography derived from UAV images. The International Archives of the Photogrammetry, Remote Sensing and Spatial Information Sciences. 2016;**XLI-B1**:1127-1134. DOI: 10.5194/isprs-archives-XLI-B1-1127-2016

[56] Yang Q, Yoo S-J. Optimal UAV path planning: Sensing data acquisition over IoT sensor networks using multi-objective bio-inspired algorithms. IEEE Access. 2018;**6**:13671-13684. DOI: 10.1109/ACCESS.2018.2812896

Chapter 4

Restitution Proposal for Medicine Pools in the Ancient City of Heraion Teichos Using Point Cloud Data

Hatice Cigdem Zagra Oz and Nese Atik

Abstract

Heraion Teichos is a Thracian city in northwestern Turkey. By using modern technologies in this ancient city, the benefits that modern technologies can provide to archeological excavations have been investigated. The main purpose of this research is to understand how modern technologies can be used to increase accuracy and precision by examining the opportunities offered by developing technology in archeological studies. How these technologies were effectively integrated into the archeological field was examined, focusing on excavation methods, digital documentation, and architectural remains of the ancient city, especially three ancient medicine production pools. This research aimed to obtain strong results by integrating traditional excavation methods with modern technology. The Heraion Teichos example demonstrates how modern technologies can be used effectively in archeological research and constitutes an example that can guide similar studies in the future.

Keywords: point cloud data, orthophoto, archeological excavations, restitution, murex

1. Introduction

Archaeology is a scientific discipline that investigates historical remnants within the scope of ancient civilizations, cultures, and civilizations, evaluating objects belonging to past civilizations. In today's context, archeological fieldwork plays a crucial role in uncovering cultural heritage assets that are under protection [1]. In this regard, it is essential to safeguard archeological sites, introduce historical values from past civilizations, and exhibit them. Therefore, meticulous efforts by the field team conducting archeological studies are necessary, with the precision required in documenting discovered objects and modeling the excavation site [2].

Technological advancements have made archeological fieldwork more effective and efficient. Various imaging techniques, especially terrestrial laser scanners, UAVs, and satellite imagery, are employed in field documentation. This allows cultural heritage assets to be digitally modeled in three dimensions, creating a permanent database that can be passed on to future generations. Furthermore, the transfer of acquired data on cultural heritage assets to digital platforms enables their three-dimensional virtual representation through multimedia tools. This situation establishes a lasting database for the transmission of past civilizations to future generations. Additionally, the use of orthophoto and 3D data facilitates the creation of restitution for the remains in archeological sites. In recent years, various studies have been conducted on three-dimensional modeling in archeological sites and the benefits of this method in digital environments. Akın and Erdogan [3] evaluated the effectiveness of unmanned aerial vehicle (UAV) Photogrammetry in archeological documentation at the Sarıkaya Roman Bath in 2022, emphasizing its potential contribution to the rapid and cost-effective documentation of historical artifacts in culturally rich regions like Turkey. Deniz et al. [4] utilized terrestrial laser methods to determine the physical characteristics of the stage wall of the Odeon structure within the ancient city of Kibrya. They highlighted that this method allowed for faster, easier, and more accurate survey drawings compared to classical methods.

In this study, an evaluation was conducted on the restitution and function of medicine production pools located in the ancient city of Heraion Teichos using 3D point cloud for exploring the different advantages provided by terrestrial laser technology. An interface program was utilized for documentation, incorporating terrestrial laser and 3D point cloud data. The assessment of pools and the surrounding wall remnants through terrestrial laser technology is a crucial stage in the restitution process. In this study, measurements were combined with the narratives of ancient authors regarding medicine production and the examination of architectural elements such as roof tiles, nails, and joints found during excavations. Literature reviews and on-site inspections were conducted to create restitution based on reliability analyses. However, archeological findings related to medicine production described in ancient written sources are very limited. Therefore, since there are no equivalents to the remains in the ancient city of Heraion Teichos, the contribution of this research to the field of archaeology is as significant as the underutilized terrestrial laser method.

2. Acropolis of ancient city of Heraion Teichos: Tekirdag

The ancient city of Heraion Teichos, located 10 km from Tekirdag province, is a Thracian city situated on the coast of the Sea of Marmara. Archeological excavations have been conducted in the region since the year 3000. The earliest architectural findings at the acropolis uncovered date back to the sixth century BC. and the latest cultural layer belongs to the first century AD [5].

Figure 1I displays the prepared site survey plan of the revealed architectural remains at the acropolis of the Ancient City Heraion Teichos using terrestrial laser scanning. The findings from archeological excavations have led to the identification of two cult areas in the acropolis. The old cult area, located at the highest point of the acropolis, is dedicated to Hera/Cybele (**Figure 1J**). The "Hera/Cybele Sacred Area/Temple," located northeast of the acropolis, was constructed with a stone cist wall and features a roof supported by wooden columns, with its existence dating back to the seventh century BC. Dedication coins from the second century BC. indicate the temple's construction during the reign of Mostis II [6]. Over time, the temple was expanded, and additional spaces were particularly added after the second century BC. A large courtyard to the west of the Hera/Cybele Cult Area/Temple and four spaces to the north were interpreted as workshops related to weaving (**Figure 1I**). Excavations in these workshops have yielded clay weights and weaving looms. Hellenistic coins

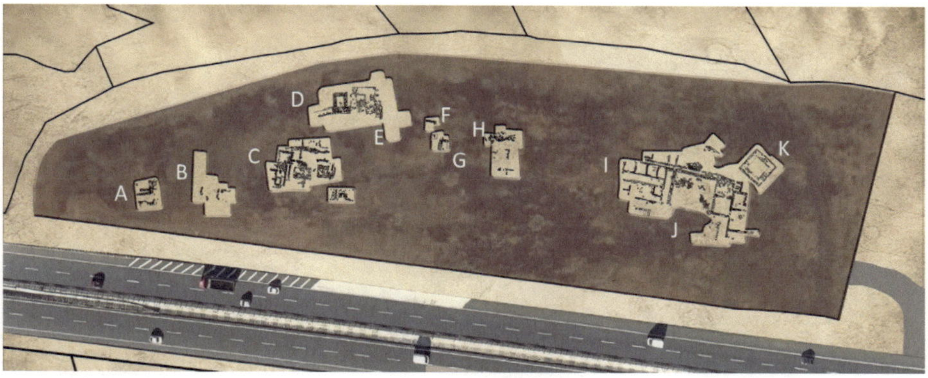

Figure 1.
A. Remains of Cult and Healing Center, B. A cult area/Temple to Zabasios, C. Remains of Cult and Healing Center: three pools, D. North gate and part of walls of the fortress, E. Necropolis, F. G. H. Control excavations, I. Workshops, J. Hera/Kybele Temple, K. Tower.

and terracotta pottery fragments were also found [7]. The Hellenistic tower was built in the thousand BC and is located northeast of the Hera/Cybele temple (**Figure 1K**). Part of the fortress walls and the northern gate were unearthed north of the acropolis (**Figure 1D**). The excavation finds lead sling bullets, bronze and iron arrowheads, and spear tips. Additionally, artifacts such as coins, terracotta figurines, and stamped amphora handles indicate that the fortress was built in the sixth century BC and was used until the period of Alexander the Great. In the Hellenistic Period, the eastern tower of the fortress gate was damaged, and the eastern part of the city wall was removed to be used as the Necropolis area (**Figure 1E**). Thracian tumuli and grave gifts were found in this necropolis. Excavations in these tombs have revealed finds such as the posthumous coin of Alexander the Great and Philip II, as well as terracotta vessels and figurine fragments [7]. After the destruction of the Hera/Kybele temple by fire, "Cult and Healing Center" was established in the west of the Acropolis (**Figure 1A–C**). Middle of the first century BC. This building complex existed until the end of the first century AD.

3. Use of medicine pools and medicine ovens in the "Cult and Healing Center"

The ruins of the "Cult and Healing Center" located to the west of the acropolis are spread over a wide area [8, 9]. Building ruins were unearthed in the southwest temple (**Figure 2a**), cult area/temple to Zabasios (**Figure 2b**), in the east of these ruins, and three medicine production pools (**Figure 2c**), in the north-east of the temple, the north of the medicine pools there are two tandoor-shaped medicine ovens and made of clay sherds.

In **Figure 2**, the orthophoto-based surveys of the three rectangular pools, which constitute the center for medicine production in the ancient city of Heraion Teichos, are presented. The geometry and dimensions of the pools are easily understood from the remains. Measurements provide accurate information about the size, depth, water circulation, and roof cover of the pools. The architectural details identified, together with archeological findings such as ancient authors' books and pottery fragments, provided information about how pools and medicine ovens were used 2000 years ago.

Figure 2.
The survey plan of the pools (a, b, c) located on the orthophoto.

There are three polls in the north of the "Cult and Healing Center's" spread area. These pools were constructed with spolia stone and used for the production of medicine (**Figure 1C**). Various medicines have been produced using "*Murex*" in and around the pools. The *Murex*, belonging to the Muricidae family, possesses therapeutic potential due to its compounds. Traditionally known for the production of ancient purple dye, this marine shellfish also forms the basis for some rare traditional medicines used for thousands of years [9]. In addition, some comprehensive studies [10–12] have documented the use of marine mollusk shells as a nutrient or raw material (**Figure 3**).

Ancient writers *Plinius, Aristotales, Aristophanes, Vitrivius,* and *Plutarchos* provide information about Murex. Its usage is quite diverse. It was used as a valuable textile dye (for the clothes of god/goddess statues, of kings), make-up, ink, and for painting [13]. The meat of *Murex Brandaris* (spikey sea snails), which is abundantly found in Heraion Teichos, was also considered a valuable food [14–18]. In the well-preserved medicine oven (**Figure 4C**), melted murex shells were identified. The first medical oven is located directly in the middle of the north side of **Figure 2b**, while the other oven is situated near the wall close to the pool in **Figure 2a**. Molten murex shells were

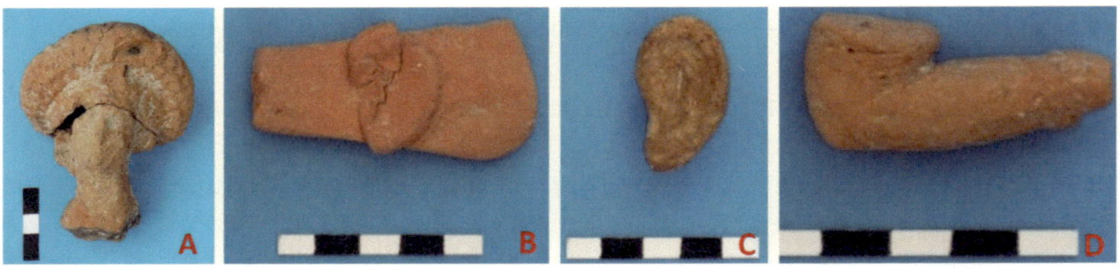

Figure 3.
Votive figurines. A. Female head, B. Ear, C. Ear, D. Arm.

Figure 4.
A. Medical utensils (forceps, spatula, ear spoon, hook, needle) B. Clay strainer, balm container, and spoon made of bone C. Murex oven.

found inside the ovens. Near the medical ovens and pools, various medical tools made of iron, lead, and bone such as forceps, spatulas, ear spoons, hooks, needles, etc. (**Figure 4A**) as well as medical vessels made of terracotta and bronze (**Figure 4B**) were discovered. The presence of diseased organs made of terracotta in this area (**Figure 3**) indicates that it was a center for both health and worship.

There are three varieties of *Murex* in Anatolia: *Murex Trunculus, Murex Brandaris, Murex Haemostoma*. All of these varieties were used as textile dyes. Purple-dark red colored textile products were obtained with this dye, called "*purpura*" in Latin. Amethist color was obtained by using three types of snails together. Color tones of purple and red were made by mixing honey, water, algae, and urine.

The textile dye must have been obtained from Murex in Heraion Teichos. Because many loom weights and spindle whorls were found during excavations. Small finds in the workshops to the west of the temple of Hera/Kybele indicate that textiles were produced. The Tumulus tomb of King Kersobleptes is 3 km far from Heraion Teichos. The king was buried here wearing his purple-colored dress. However, the three pools we examined cannot be paint pools. To obtain dye, *Murexes* are kept in warm water with their shells.

Murex flesh and shells are separated into three medicine-making pools. Medicine was made by melting murex shells in the ovens north of the pools. According to the ancient writer Plinius, murex was pressed, burned, and melted, then mixed with lard and honey and applied to the skin as an ointment against burns. This burn cream was called "όζνγγία." Melted murex was ground to make a powder called κηρύκες, which was used to clean teeth. In two pools in Heraion Teichos (**Figure 4a,b**), murex flesh was separated in the pool, and the shells were melted in the nearby furnaces to make medicine. Pools a and b have roofs over them because they work under the sun for long periods of time. The ancient writer Xenocrates says that murex meat flesh was tied to swollen muscles and used in treatment. The meat separated in these pools was probably used in this way.

The flesh, secretion, and also shells, of *Murex* have been used as medicine. Ancient writer *Hippocrates* says that its secretion solves digestive problems. *Plinius* said that its secretion was useful against some types of poison. The third pool, which is smaller than the other, has no roof (**Figure 4c**). Cooking pots and traces of ash found around this pool suggest the making of different medicines, especially those that require cooking. For example, the ancient writer *Dioskurides* said that deep-fried murex flesh was a cure for baldness. Therefore, the third, smaller pool must have been used for processing murex flesh. For example, a swollen liver was treated by soaking the flesh of *Murex* in vinegar. The flesh separated in other pools was probably washed in this small pool and then used for cutting, cooking, and storage. A *pithos* (storage container) buried in the ground was found in one of the chambers. To the west of the pools. A pottery sherd with an inscription "ΛΟΥΦΑΡΜΑ" (farma = medicine) written on it also indicates that medicine was stored.

4. Terrestrial laser scanning (TLS) method

Laser scanning technology used in the form of LIDAR, which stands for Light Detection and Ranging, is an active remote sensing technology that produces high-accuracy three-dimensional (3D) data using a laser beam [19]. Laser scanning technologies involve the emission of laser beams onto a surface or area through a laser scanning device, enabling the acquisition of three-dimensional (3D) point cloud data for that space. The inception and design of this technology have been made possible through interdisciplinary collaborations among electrical, computer, geodetic, and photogrammetric engineers. Leveraging the characteristics of high-power laser radiation, short pulses, or modulation, terrestrial laser scanning proves advantageous for measurements [20, 21].

Research in the field has been focused on accuracy analysis, and calibration reports elucidating the relationship between reflected laser intensity and surface reflection, factors influencing the accuracy of laser scanners, employing the Lambert reflection model [22]. Terrestrial laser scanning technology, with a measurement accuracy of 99.9% (±2 mm) in complex geometries, offers numerous advantages, including cost reduction, workforce efficiency, time savings, versatile data utilization and sharing, obtaining detailed and comprehensive data in a single session for transformative use, and enabling measurements in hazardous or inaccessible areas where conventional measurement becomes challenging [23].

4.1 3D point cloud image

Laser scanning technology used in the form of LIDAR, which stands for light detection and ranging, is an active remote sensing technology that produces high-accuracy three-dimensional (3D) data using a laser beam [24]. Terrestrial laser scanners can generate a point cloud with X, Y, and Z coordinates for any desired object. From the obtained point cloud, a 3D model of the object can be created [25]. Laser scanning technology is a system that enables the representation of object surfaces with 3D coordinates. Essentially, the distance between the scanner and a specific point on the object's surface is determined with high accuracy by measuring the round-trip time of the laser signal [26]. According to the summarized fieldwork presented in the diagram on the left side in **Figure 5**, session locations and scanning parameters are crucial.

4.2 Orthophoto

Laser scanning technology used in the form of LIDAR, which stands for Light Detection and Ranging, is an active remote sensing technology that produces

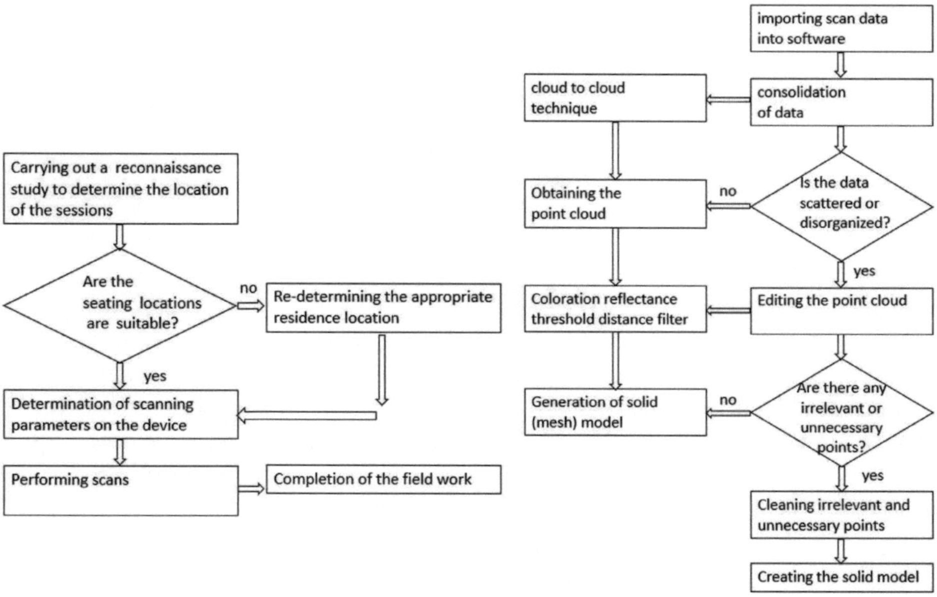

Figure 5.
Fieldwork workflow diagram (left) workflow diagram for Scene (right) [27].

high-accuracy three-dimensional (3D) data using a laser beam [24]. An orthophoto is an aerial photograph or satellite image that corrects for terrain elevation, camera tilt, and lens distortion. It produces a map-like image, enabling accurate measurements of distances, angles, and areas. Its applications include engineering, planning, design, and map production. Data sources include aerial photographs and satellite images. The quality of an orthophoto depends on factors such as operator skill, parameter selection, and the digital elevation model used. In particular, the planimetric density of the digital elevation model controls the accuracy of the surface model [28]. In **Figure 5**, the diagram on the right side schematically illustrates the workflow in the Faro Scene software.

4.3 Use of orthophoto in archeological sites

LIDAR scanner methods are divided into two: TLS (Terrestrial LIDAR System) and ALS (Airborne LIDAR System) [29]. In general, TLS (Terrestrial LIDAR System) terrestrial LIDAR systems are used for modeling in archeological excavation sites. In tasks such as scanning objects containing complex geometries, scanning surfaces from a single point may not provide accurate and usable data. In such cases, scanning should be done with rays sent from different points, and then these scans should be combined and transferred to the geodetic coordinate system. Computer aided design (CAD) software is used to integrate scanning data with spatial data [23].

5. Documentation of Heraion Teichos Ancient City with terrestrial laser scanning

For the production of 3D models, the laser scanner device used is the Faro Focus M 70 model, manufactured by the laser scanner manufacturers Faro, with its basic technical specifications presented in **Table 1**.

Feature	Value
Scan count	188 pcs
Resolution	¼ pix
Quality	4x pix
HDR	3x pix

Table 1.
The parameters used in scanning [30].

Heraion Teichos Ancient City covers an area of approximately 26,954 m^2, and a total of 188 scans, capturing 1,446,050,556 points, were conducted at seven different locations. The scans were merged with a precision of 2.95 mm using the cloud-to-cloud method in the SCENE 2022 program. Subsequently, they were overlaid onto images to create a point cloud. The scans were performed on sunny days, specifically on October 5–8, 2023, using a laser scanner mounted on a tripod.

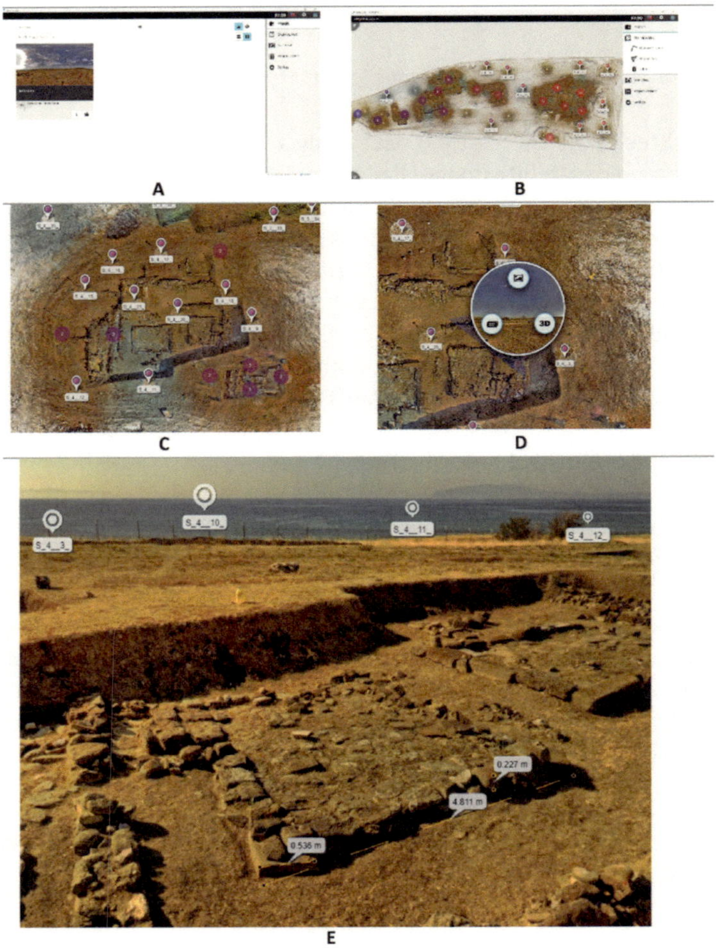

Figure 6.
The user interface of the Scene 2go program.

After the data collection phase in the field, the acquired data in ".fls" format is transferred to the Scene program, which is Faro's software, and the process of coloring the points is carried out. Following the completion of the coloring, the data undergoes the referencing and merging process. Subsequently, point clouds are generated. Two-dimensional orthophoto images are obtained from the created point clouds in the form of plans, cross-sections, and elevations. Additionally, for the support of photogrammetric work, the point cloud is exported in pts. format. The data obtained from the Scene software, with its high resolution and byte size, complicates the end user's work and data flow. Therefore, to facilitate data transfer to the end user and enable the user to work with low bytes, the data exported from the Faro Scene software is converted into the Scene 2go program, whose working principle is summarized in **Figure 6**.

The data transferred to the end user enables two separate versions, one for the Mac and one for the Windows operating system, within a folder. **Figure 6A** is the project entry screen, providing access to all session locations and site plans, as shown in **Figure 6B** through the photograph on the left. The session icons include elevation classification. This classification is expressed with a color scale ranging between blue and red. The location information in red indicates higher elevations, while approaching the blue color tone signifies a lower elevation. In **Figure 6C**, the site plan makes our session locations more distinct, and the number of sessions in that area can be clearly seen. When clicking on the location marker in **Figure 6D**, visual data of the scanned area, point cloud data, and session recording information can be accessed. **Figure 6E** shows the visual data and panoramic view of the session that we access when clicked. Due to the presence of point data in the background of the photo, measurements can be made accurately using the points, and the area can be calculated correctly.

6. Restitution proposal of medicine pools and medicine furnaces in the "Cult and Healing Center"

For the restitution in the archeological field, a detailed on-site examination is essential. The original construction traces on the remnants of the structure and the positions of the fallen stones assist in determining their original locations. When evaluated from this perspective, terrestrial laser scanning enables this examination through 3D point cloud and matched photographs, supporting the on-site investigation. Additionally, the readily accessible data facilitates the tracking of traces.

In the first century BC, ancient pools were found along the Mediterranean and Aegean coasts. Although their sizes and functions vary, most facilities can be easily identified by the presence of fairly standardized pools. Usually constructed with square or rectangular walls, often partially collapsed or protruding, these pools are observed to be coated with opus signinum, a waterproof mortar mixture of lime and small tiles or ceramic particles. Rubblestone is commonly used as a building material. The shell residues within the pools indicate that these facilities could be used for cleaning, washing, or extracting shells and dyeing clothes [31]. Additionally, Vitruvius notes that these shells were broken into pieces with iron tools and referred to as "tire" due to the odor in cities engaged in dye production [32]. Research on ancient pools suggests that these structures could be associated with functions such as dye production, raw material processing, and the production of food and medicine.

In **Figure 7**, similar examples of recent periods are examined. The pool numbered 1 in **Figure 7** was uncovered in 2016 by removing collapsed roof tiles and wall rubble,

No	1	2	3
Period	early 3rd century BC	1rd-2rd centuries A.D.	1rd century A.D.
Location	Citadel of Ancient Paphos	Torregarcía (Almería,Spain)	Lixus Morocco
Photograph			

Figure 7.
Comparative period analysis.

revealing a layer of purple shells. After the analysis of these layers, it was suggested that the pool was used for the production of purple dye. After removing the layer of purple shells, brick tiles on the floor of the pool were revealed [33]. In the area where the pool numbered 2 in **Figure 7** is located, Roman ceramics and a layer of shells were found. Laboratory analysis of the shells indicated that Hexaplex trunculus dominated with a percentage of 93%, and this type of seashell was noted to be the best species for producing purple dye [34]. The pool numbered 3 in **Figure 7** is reported to have been used as a fish salting facility. These areas, called Catariae, can be found outdoors or in enclosed spaces with doors and windows for ventilation. These pools are often used as a section where marine resources are washed and cleaned or where shells and dyes are prepared. Sometimes, they are used to reduce the structure of sauces, increase the temperature of the dye mixture, or obtain salt from seawater. Additionally, at sites with cetariae in the Northwest Maghreb, murex/purpura shells are frequently observed. These seashells are likely used in the production of various salted sauces in the region, along with other types of seashells such as clams and oysters (**Figure 8**) [31].

Measurements provide precise information about architectural details. The width of the pool in **Figure 4a** ranges from 4.80 to 6.75 m, with a maximum depth of 0.60 m. The width of the pool in **Figure 4b** ranges from 4.80 to 4.70 m, with a maximum depth of 0.30 m. The width of the pool in **Figure 4c** ranges from 2.10 to 2.50 m, with a maximum depth of 0.40 m. In some corners of the pools, there are cubic and cylindrical column bases with a hole in the middle, approximately 0.33 m in height and 0.23 m in width. Stone column bases belong to ancient buildings. In fact, old architectural material (spolia) was used in the pools and all the structures around them such as an architrave fragment, an inscribed sill, etc. Additionally, the roof of the pool on the west side shows that it is supported by four columns, and the roof of the pool on the east side is supported by eight columns.

During the excavation, a significant number of iron nails were found beneath the tiles, indicating a wooden structure. The roofs covered with tiles were likely transported by stone-based, wooden columns, as evidenced by the column bases with holes in the corners of the pools. Wooden columns should have been attached to these stones with a metal rod through the round holes in the middle. Literature research also supports this [35]. Bases were found at the four corners of the western pool, but only one has survived to the present day (**Figure 9**). The base, wooden post, and details of the roof covering the pool are depicted in **Figure 10**. It is believed that the

Figure 8.
Illustration of ancient pools (a, b, c), murex ovens (d, e), and water pipe (f).

Figure 9.
Stone base (above – 2006, below – 2023).

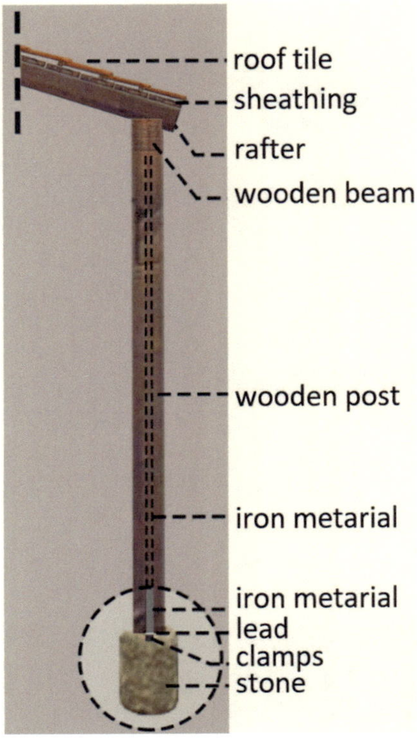

Figure 10.
Wooden column detail.

ancient pools had roofs covered with Laconian-type tiles, measuring approximately 50x35x4cm, with dimensions similar to those of the pools.

On the western side of the pools, there are adobe structures with rubble stone foundations. It is understood that these structures contain frescoes in their interiors. In the western chambers, a large number of murex shells and pithos buried in the ground were found in one of the chambers. These chambers are likely storage areas for drugs and drug materials. In the northern chambers, there were baked clay pots and numerous lamps. The lamps suggest that activities continued in the areas around the pools until late hours.

The water brought to the pools was partially conveyed over the remains of the Hera/Kybele Temple through terracotta water pipes (outer diameter 10.5 cm, wall thickness 2 cm) inclined westward (**Figure 8f**). The clean water, passing over the remains of the Hera/Kybele Temple, reaches the pools with an approximate elevation difference of 6 meters. At the point where the clean water pipes continue in front of the temple ruins, the water is filtered by passing through a jar, and a round marble cover is placed on top of the jar. To the east of this jar, a stone trough has been found. The opening here should have been made to adjust the water pressure and/or to clean large stones that may have mixed into the water.

In addition to the terracotta water pipes that conveyed clean water from the Hera/Kybele Temple in an east-west direction to the medicine pools in the west of the acropolis, it has been determined that there are other clean water pipes extending in the north-south and west directions. In a borehole in the center of the acropolis, it can be observed that the water, filtered through a jar, is connected to the south with two pipes and to the west with one pipe. The fact that the pipes connecting in the north-south direction also connect to the east-west water pipes indicates that almost the entire acropolis was involved in health-related activities.

The entry point of the water to the small pool, which was uncovered in 2023, has been determined to be from the east, similar to the eastern one of the two adjacent pools that received water directed to the west. It is observed that the wastewater from this small pool, located southeast of the two large pools, is directed to the west and connected to the wastewater channel made of large flat stones, which is directed south like the other pools. Traces from the structure, literature research, and period examples support the proposed restoration of the ancient medicine pool (**Figure 8**).

7. Conclusion

Antique cities are archeological areas with extensive surface areas, and the remnants of structures and other cultural artifacts are often found scattered in these areas. These cities encompass large architectural complexes constructed in different periods throughout history. In this study, terrestrial laser scanning (TLS) and three-dimensional point cloud data have facilitated the continuous tracking of architectural remains and the understanding of material continuity on a digital platform without physically traversing distances. The architecture of the ancient pools in the Heraion Teichos Antique City, their relationship with each other, and the connections between the water distribution pipes and the pools in the city were analyzed and interpreted using the Scene 2go program, where meshed photos based on three-dimensional point cloud data were observed. Moreover, due to the detailed information provided by TLS and three-dimensional point cloud data on the material, texture, dimensions, shape, and deterioration of archeological remains, a comprehensive understanding was achieved. These data facilitated undeniable convenience in creating scaled and measured illustrations for the restitution of structures.

With terrestrial laser scanning (TLS), the structures in the Heraion Teichos Ancient City have been rapidly and accurately scanned, resulting in time and labor savings compared to traditional measurement methods. The obtained data can be utilized for the detailed examination of the topographic structure of the area, understanding terrain changes, elevation differences, and other topographic features. The high-precision point data can determine the geographical location of the archeological site and facilitate coordination between different data sets. Archeologists can better understand the overall structure of the area before excavation with the 3D data obtained, allowing them to optimize excavation strategies.

In conclusion, precise scanning data provides a more comprehensive, fast, and effective research and documentation process in archeological sites. This allows researchers an opportunity for more in-depth study and contributes to the preservation of documented (digital documentation) historical structures for future generations.

Conflict of interest

The authors declare no conflict of interest.

Notes/thanks/other declarations

This study was supported within the scope of the Istanbul Rumeli University Scientific Research Projects under the project number "BAP2023001." We would like to express our gratitude to the Istanbul Rumeli University Scientific Research Commission, to Sahin Tas, a graduate student at Istanbul Rumeli University, for his contribution to the survey drawings, and to Lidart Company.

Author details

Hatice Cigdem Zagra Oz* and Nese Atik
Istanbul Rumeli University, Istanbul, Turkey

*Address all correspondence to: hcigdem.zagra@rumeli.edu.tr

References

[1] Alptekin A, Celik MO, Dogan Y, Yakar M. Illustrating of a landslide site with photogrammetric and LIDAR methods. In: El-Askary H, Karakus M, Abiddin Erguler Z, Chamine HI, editors. Research Developments in Geotechnics, Geo-Informatics and Remote Sensing. Cham: Springer International Publishing; 2022. pp. 303-305

[2] Demirkesen AC, Ozludemir MT, Demir HM. Preservation of historical and cultural heritage in the case of Cappadocia and the powers and responsibilities of survey engineers in these processes. In: TMMOB Chamber of Surveying and Cadastral Engineers 10th Turkish Mapping Scientific and Technical Congress; 28 March–1 April 2005; Ankara. pp. 1-10

[3] Akın ES, Erdogan A. Documentation in archaeological sites with unmanned aerial vehicles (UAV): Example of Sarıkaya Roman Bath (Therma basilica). Suleyman Demirel University Institute of Science and Technology Journal. 2022;**26**(3):335-343

[4] Deniz S, Oktem S, Kirbas I, Tarkan D. Use of spatial/terrestrial laser scanners in determining the physical features of archaeological sites: Example of the stage wall of the Odeon structure of the Ancient City of Kibrya. Mehmet Akif Ersoy University Institute of Science and Technology Journal. 2017;**8**(Suppl. 1):211-217

[5] Atik N. The magnificent Temple of the Thracian mother goddess in the Ancient City of Tekirdag Heraion Teichos. In: Ureten H, Sina A, editors. Tekirdag. A Gift to the 100th Anniversary of its Establishment. İstanbul: Karadeniz Book Ltd. Sti; 2023. pp. 9-14

[6] Yagız MO. The coins of the thracian king mostis. In: Fourth International Forum of Calligraphy,Writing and Inscriptions in the World throughout the Ages Coins in the World; 16-18 March 2009. Alexandria: Abgadiyat; 2010. pp. 65-70

[7] Atik N. Thracians and the Ancient City of Heraion Teichos in Tekirdag. Archeology and Art. 2016;**152**:75-86

[8] Atik N. Tekirdag Karaevlialtı ancient Heraion Teichos excavation. In: T.R. Ministry of Culture and Tourism XLI, International Excavation Research Archaeometry Symposium; 23-27 May 2022. Denizli, Ankara: Ministry of Culture and Tourism; 2019, 2022. pp. 369-378

[9] Atik N. Two important monuments in the ancient city of Heraion Teichos: The sanctuary of Hera/Kybele and the sanctuary of the god of health. In: Thirteenth International Congress of Thracology Kazanlak, 3-7 September 2017. Vol. 2. Sofia: Ancient Thrace: Myth And Reality; 2022. pp. 21-30

[10] Benkendorff K, Rudd D, Nongmaithem BD, Liu L, Young F, Edwards V, et al. Are the traditional medical uses of Muricidae molluscs substantiated by their pharmacological properties and bioactive compounds? Marine Drugs. 2015;**13**(8):5237-5275. DOI: 10.3390/md13085237

[11] Shackleton JC, Van Andel TH. Prehistoric shore environments, shellfish availability, and shellfish gathering at Franchthi, Greece. Geoarchaeology. 1986;**1**(2):127-143

[12] Karali L. The seashells of Maroulas, Kythnos. In: Sampson A, Kaczanowska M, Kozlowski JK, editors.

The Prehistory of the Island of Kythnos (Cyclades, Greece) and the Mesolithic Settlement at Maroulas. Krakow: The Polish Academy of Arts and Sciences; 2010. pp. 147-149

[13] Yavsan C. Sea Shells Found in Chalcolithic Smintheion (Gulpınar) Excavations. Çanakkale: Troia Foundation Publications; 2013. p. 111

[14] Eyuboglu O, Okaygun I, Yaras F. Woll Dyeing with Natural Dyes. 1st ed. İstanbul: Ozkur Publisher; 1983. p. 138

[15] Keller O. The Ancient Animal World. 2nd ed. Vol. 2. Leipzig: W. Engelmann; 1980. p. 568

[16] Herrmann F. Milesian Purple. Istanbul News. 1975:141-147

[17] Rackham H. Pliny's Natural History. Vol. 1-5, 9. London: Harvard University Press; 1949-1954. p. 230

[18] Schneider. Realencyclopedia of Classical Antiquity. Stuttgart: Metzler; 1959

[19] Gungor M. Examining the use of terrestrial laser scanners in archaeological sites. Turkey Lidar Magazine. 2022;**4**(2):85-90

[20] Ready JF. Industrial Applications of Lasers. Elsevier; 1997. p. 588

[21] Wehr A, Lohr U. Airborne laser scanning—An introduction and overview. ISPRS Journal of Photogrammetry and Remote Sensing. 1999;**54**(2-3):68-82

[22] Hancock JA. Laser intensity-based obstacle detection and tracking [PhD. thesis]. Pittsburgh: Robotics Institute, Carnegie Mellon University; 1999

[23] Reshetyuk Y. Investigation and calibration of pulsed time-of-flight terrestrial laser scanners [PhD. thesis]. KTH, School of Architecture and the Built Environment (ABE), Royal Institute of Technology (KTH); 2006

[24] Erisir Z. Classification of LIDAR data with point-based classification method [thesis]. Yıldız Technical University, Institute of Science, Department of Surveying Engineering, Remote Sensing and GIS Program; 2015

[25] Elkhrachy I, Niemeier W. Optimization and strength aspects for geo-referencing data with Terresterial laser scanner systems. In: 3rd IAG7/12th FIG Symposium; 22-24 May 2006; Baden. pp. 1-10

[26] Akyol O, Duran Z. Low-cost laser scanning system design. Journal of Russian Laser Research. 2014;**35**:244-251. DOI: 10.1007/s10946-014-9419-2

[27] Yakar I, Çelik MO, Sng H, Bilgi S. Comparison of different software in cultural heritage documentation studies: Obelisk (Theodosius obelisk) example. Geomatics. 2021, 2021;**6**(3):217-226. DOI: 10.29128/geomatik.761475

[28] Ayhan E, Erden O, Atay G, Tunc E. Digital orthophoto generation with aerial photos and satellite images and analyzing of factors which affect accuracy. In: Shaping the Change, XXIII International FIG Congress. Munich; 2006. pp. 552-565. Available from: https://www.oicrf.org/documents/40950/43224/Digital+orthophoto+generation+with+aerial+photos+and+satellite+images+and+analyzing+of+factors+which+affect+accuracy.pdf/7f030532-73c5-081d-3c45-0c5edec69c28?t=1510174503870

[29] Polat N, Uysal M. A general overview of air laser scanning system, application areas and software used.

Afyon Kocatepe University Journal of Science and Engineering Sciences. 2016;**16**(3):679-692

[30] Tekin E. Lidart Education and Construction Industry. İstanbul: Trade Limited Company; 2023

[31] Trakadas A. Fish-Salting in the Northwest Maghreb in Antiquity: A Gazetteer of Sites and Resources. Oxford: Archaeopress Publishing Ltd; 2016. p. 177

[32] Vitruvius P. Vitruvius Architectura (Illustrated). US: Amazon Digital Services; 2021. p. 409

[33] Lacovou M, Mylona D. Purple Dye Production under Royal Management: Evidence from the Cypro-Classical Citadel of Ancient Paphos Notebook of the Center for Cypriot Studies. Vol. 492019. pp. 167-178. DOI: 10.4000/cchyp.586

[34] Lopez-Medina MJ et al. Non-invasive prospection techniques in the Cabo de Gata-Níjar Natural Park (Almería, Spain): Torregarcía's site. Land. 2023;**12**(2):304-326. DOI: 10.3390/land12020304

[35] Tokoz OD, Ipekoglu B. Anastelosis of Greco-Roman temple remains in Western Anatolia: Principles, implementations and assessment. Conservation and Management of Archaeological Sites. 2020;**22**(1-2):1-37. DOI: 10.1080/13505033.2021.1882094